A SENSE
of
PRESENCE

A SENSE
of
PRESENCE

Edwin F. White

Christian Communications
P.O. Box 150
Nashville, TN 37202

Published by Christian Communications
A division of the Gospel Advocate Co.
P.O. Box 150, Nashville, TN 37202

Cover by Southern Designs

ISBN 0-89225-357-6

Contents

To my wife,
Pat,
In whose lovely life
I first caught a glimpse of God.

Foreword

I often have been perplexed by the ungodly lives of people and their total disregard of what God wants them to do. I would think, "How can they live like that?" or "How can they do things they know are wrong?" I couldn't understand why they would do something when they knew it was in direct opposition to God. I now understand.

I also have wondered why people could be so disinterested in religious matters. I knew they were living a lifestyle that was what they preferred, but it seemed to me that it ought to bother them that they weren't Christians. I now understand.

What helped me to understand this disregard of spiritual matters was that it never occurred to them to even consider God if there was a conflict of wills—there was no sense of God's presence. God's presence should have been so strong in their minds that they wouldn't have dared go against His will.

A Sense of Presence will help you to be concerned about your relationship with God. You will see that in everything you do, there needs to be a sense of the presence of God.

Once in a great while an author and a book comes along that you can get excited about. Edwin White and *A Sense of Presence* is one of those instances. But, most of all, you will have a greater sense of the presence of God because of Edwin White's having written this book.

Don Humphrey

Introduction

Recent studies by time-management specialists reveal that during a lifetime, the average American spends six months sitting at red lights, eight months opening junk mail, one year searching for things that are lost, four years cleaning house, five years waiting in lines, six years eating, and seven years in the bathroom.

Brushing teeth, eating, waiting in lines, sitting at red lights, opening mail, and cleaning house are activities you tend to view in isolation. When, however, you think about the time consumed by demands of things small in themselves but not in their accumulation, you are overwhelmed with a feeling that insignificant things are nibbling us to death.

Much of what you do, of course, cannot be avoided. You cannot neglect personal hygiene just because, on average, you spend seven years of your life in the bathroom. You can, and must, understand that life measures itself by the accumulation of small activities, and you must establish priorities for a wiser use of time.

What worries me most is the feeling that frivolous things gnaw our spiritual lives to death.

Modern Christianity engrosses itself in a world of anxious activity that consumes time and attention. We are so busy building churches, administering programs, and managing our corporate assets that we have no time to pursue a personal relationship with God. The cumulative effect of less important activities robs us of time to develop a greater awareness of Divine Presence. As a result, God, who alone can satisfy the human soul, is lost to his people.

The purpose of this book is to help God's dying children find renewed life in a greater awareness of their heavenly Father. Although it may be true that eternity will be the supreme manifestation of God, it is possible to see and hear God now if one has a well-developed sense of spiritual sight. For the one who is spiritually sensitive, even the invisible things of God are "clearly seen" (Romans 1:20).

The modern church is at its present low estate because it is unaware of God. Conformity to God is possible only through individual communion with him. Moses looked with loving eyes upon the glory of God and was unconsciously transformed to its very image. Moses "was not aware that his face was radiant," but it had become a luminous reflection of God's glory (Exodus 34:29). This is the only means of transfiguration—to draw so near to the heart of God that his light makes our whole being shine.

This generation of Christians needs transfiguration. We must come in touch with God. Only by transfiguration can we create a moral atmosphere in which selfishness and sin cannot live and where joy reigns supreme.

My prayer is that this book will help God's people become more aware of his presence and, in that awareness, seek an intimate communion which transforms us and brings joy to the heart of God.

Edwin F. White

CHAPTER 1

Activity Without Insight

The attitude of pessimism is not new. Plato, for instance, thought it possible for society to achieve justice and happiness, but he imposed harsh conditions for their attainment and was pessimistic in his view that happiness eludes all but a select few. The decline and fall of the Roman Empire gave birth to a deep pessimism evoked by the death of a historical order that was thought to be universal and eternal. Scholars have long regarded the Middle Ages as clouded with pessimism.

In modern times, Clarence Darrow, Leo Tolstoy and Arthur Schopenhauer developed well-defined philosophies of pessimism. Darrow compared life to a "ship on the sea, tossed by every wave and by every wind; a ship headed for no port and no harbor, with no rudder, no compass, no pilot; simply floating for a time, then lost in the waves."[1]

In "A Confession," Tolstoy wrote, "Today or tomorrow sickness will come to those I love or to me; nothing will remain but stench and worms. Sooner or later my affairs, whatever they may be, will be forgotten and I shall not exist. Then why go on making the effort?"[2]

Schopenhauer felt the world should not exist. He concluded, "We have not to rejoice but rather to mourn at the existence of the world . . . ." "The world," said Schopenhauer, "is something which ought not to be."[3]

When pessimism results from critical analysis about the relative impact of good and evil in human life, it becomes a true philosophy. I believe however, that the gloominess of this present age does not owe its existence to a

1

well-formulated theory, but to an emotional response to the seeming unsolvable problems of life. In other words, modern pessimism is primarily a personal opinion or attitude, not a philosophical theory.

If pessimism seems more intense now than ever before, it is because of a perception that no age, like the present, has had to face so many difficult problems. The world continues to reel under the pressure of unanswered questions and unresolved problems of recent origin. Besides the problems of the bomb, drugs, alcohol, the Cold War, communism, poverty and the environment, we now have the added worry of AIDS, which threatens to touch, directly or indirectly, the lives of everyone. Try as we may, we seem unable to find solutions to the frustrating problems of the modern world. In despair, many have concluded that there are no answers to the questions that perplex our age.

Because of the seeming hopelessness of this age, the church has a glorious opportunity. The Christian message of hope is precisely what the world needs to hear. Presented effectively, the offer of a "peace that passes understanding" would attract the worried billions of this generation like a magnet.

Unfortunately, the church stumbles under the weight of its own brand of pessimism. We poison ourselves with the "invisible, odorless gas of apathy." The problem is not that God is dead, but that many Christians are dead.

God and Radical Theology

As early as 1802, G.W.F. Hegel, a German philosopher and theologian, announced that God was culturally dead. Friedrich Nietzsche gave God a funeral eighty years later. Nietzsche, son of a Lutheran minister, rejected all religions, but held a special contempt for Christianity. Nietzsche thought Christ was pure—free of resentment—but profoundly pathological. The disciples misunderstood Jesus, and from the start the church was in opposition to Jesus' spirit. Christianity, as Nietzsche saw it, was deeply resentful of unbelievers, was hostile to the world, and was a movement in which bitterness was central to a so-called religion of love. Both Buddhism, which Nietzsche considered a religion of weariness, and Hinduism, which he considered objectionable because of its treatment of the untouchables, were preferred to Christianity. The Christian idea of God was unworthy of belief. Nietzsche declared that the death of God was not only desirable, but a cultural fact. He announced that God, man's greatest danger, was in the grave. Man is now liberated.

Some 60 years after Nietzsche's death, Thomas Altizer and William Hamilton, American theologians most commonly associated with the death of God movement, revived Nietzsche's theme, inspiring "the death of God" controversy of the 1960s. Few discussions ever attracted so much popular attention or aroused such passions. The radical theologians introduced us to new terms like "Christian atheism" and "radical Christianity." They told us about God's death for modern man and that it is no longer possible to trust in a personal, transcendent, caring God of Judeo-Christian tradition. The theologians advised believers to trust their own ability to solve problems without reference to God. They preached that Christians should welcome the death of God as a redemptive act which frees us from bondage to an oppressive deity.

The Church Impotent

Announcements of God's death, however, were premature, and atheism remains a minority belief. The problem is that the very children of God who resisted the conclusions of the radical theologians, remain, for the most part, without a personal awareness of God's presence. The precious church of Christ on the whole is spiritually impoverished. I cannot see the slightest indication that most Christians of this age know God in personal experience. As a result, we have a God with whom we do not communicate, who cannot commune with us or have an impact in our lives and ministry. God is alive, but he might as well be dead.

In 25 years of preaching, the most common complaint

3

I have heard from Christians is, "Life just doesn't mean anything anymore." This generation of Christians has a terminal illness—boredom. The churches are feverishly excited, but self-indulgent, dispassionate, and weary of self and others. We are busy, but time hangs heavily in our hands. We need to be awakened from our barren, monotonous and deathlike existence.

In response to my announcement that the church is impotent, some undoubtedly will take offense. Others will offer rebuttal. Some will point to the church's many programs and activities in an effort to prove that the Christian community involves itself with the needs of people. I agree that the church has more programs and corporate assets than ever before in its history. However, there is a difference between activity and spirituality. Programs, methods and outward forms can never satisfy a longing heart. Only God can satisfy the soul. Just because the modern church occupies itself with a world of nervous activities that fill time and attention is no proof of spiritual life.

> *The problem is not that God is dead, but that many Christians are dead.*

Excitement Without Enthusiasm

Jesus said that the greatest commandment is to love God with all the heart, mind, soul and strength. Jesus says the most important business of life is to have a hunger for God that always remains unsatisfied. We must thirst for God as the "deer pants for streams of water" (Psalm 42:1,2). We have only one task as Christians— to love God above all.

Passion for God, however, is lost to the church in this generation. As a result, we are dead. The churches are astir, but they have no spiritual ardor. We have managed to acquire only an excess of excitement while retaining a deficiency of genuine enthusiasm. Enthusiasm is spiritual, serious and self-controlled. Excitement is outward, extravagant and often tumultuous. Excitement is of impulse,

4

but enthusiasm is of conviction. Excitement is merely the glow; enthusiasm is the fire.

The sad truth is that this church age is totally oblivious to the absence of fire. Much of what is seen in the church today is nothing more than a frenzied excitement which succeeds only in exhausting the mind, leaving it shriveled and spent. Instead of genuine enthusiasm, we see only a fanatical sensationalism. Our aim is to pursue the presence of God, but we have forgotten what our aim is while redoubling our efforts. We are too busy building churches to fulfill our purpose, and as Lewis Carroll put it:

> Where life becomes a spasm,
> and history a whiz:
> If that's not sensational,
> I don't know what is.

The average Christian today is like a person driving down a freeway in heavy traffic at a high rate of speed. Little time is given to reading signs and taking directions. As a result, many become lost in pathless places. Motion has no value unless it gets us somewhere. A few thoughtless people believe that movement is beneficial, even if it is in the wrong direction. Richard Cumberland concluded that "It is better to wear out than to rust out." A line from Shakespeare comes even nearer the truth: "I were better to be eaten to death with rust than to be scoured to nothing with perpetual motion."

"Nothing," said Johann Goethe, the 18th century German poet, dramatist, novelist and scientist, "is so terrible as activity without insight." Activity without insight is a common failure of modern Christianity. We occupy ourselves with the endless, meaningless, unanticipated demands of church life, and the necessary activities of spiritual development go neglected. We

I cannot see the slightest indication that most Christians of this age know God in personal experience.

are too busy to pursue God, who, alone, can satisfy the longing of the human heart. The problem with modern Christians is that they travel the low road. The church

5

has fallen into a dull routine of managing its programs, committees and corporate assets. I can't help thinking of the old German proverb which asks, "What is the use of running when we are not on the right road?"

Seeing God

Believers must see God more clearly and love him more deeply. We will fulfill our purpose only when we make God real by a continuous pursuit of his presence. God wants his people to seek him, and to those who "love his appearing," he comes, not in "clouds descending," but in the impact of his spiritual presence.

Jesus announced himself to John as the one "who is, and was, and who is to come" (Revelation 1:8). In other words, Jesus is Lord of the past, present and future—the Christ who came and remains and is yet to come.

The Christian community is familiar with the Christ "who was"—the historical Jesus. Those who knew Jesus in the flesh testified that they had seen with their eyes and touched with their hands "the Word of Life" (1 John 1:1). To his disciples, Jesus became a personal, precious experience. True believers accept the testimony of those who personally knew the Lord and respect him as the central figure in history.

The church also is accustomed to thinking of the Christ who is to come. We often hear sermons about the second coming of Christ.

But what of the Christ who remains? Christians seem strangely unaware of the Presence, living as if God were not here at all. Jehovah is not an absentee God, sitting idle, just outside the universe; he isn't, as one philosopher suggested, "absent-minded." Rather, "in him we live, and move, and have our being" (Acts 17:28). The Lord promised, "I will never leave thee, nor forsake thee" (Hebrews 13:5). Therefore, we may say boldly, "The Lord is my helper; I will not be afraid. What can man do to me?" (Hebrews 13:6).

Divine Presence

God always has been present among his people. Adam

6

and Eve enjoyed a sweet, intimate relationship with God in Eden. We remember Abraham, Isaac and Jacob, not for their mighty swords, but because they were God's intimate friends.

God promised Moses, "My presence shall go with thee, and I will give thee rest" (Exodus 33:14). When the children of Israel were about to enter the Promised Land, Moses reminded them that because God loved their forefathers, he "chose their descendants after them, he brought you out of Egypt by his Presence . . ." (Deuteronomy 4:37). Moses also exhorted the people, "But if from there you seek the Lord your God, you will find him if you look for him with all your heart and with all your soul" (Deuteronomy 4:29).

Upon its completion and dedication, the tabernacle filled with the glory of Jehovah. God's cloud was over the tabernacle by day, and fire was in the cloud by night to lead Israel throughout all their journeys (Exodus 40:34-38).

Because Jehovah for centuries "walked in a tent and in a tabernacle," David wanted to build a house for Jehovah's dwelling place (2 Samuel 7:5-7). Solomon eventually built the temple on Mount Moriah, which is where God had revealed himself to Abraham. Upon dedication of the temple, the fire, a symbol of Jehovah's presence and power, descended from Heaven and consumed the sacrifices on the altar, "and the glory of the Lord filled the temple. The priests could not enter the temple of the Lord because the glory of the Lord filled it" (2 Chronicles 7:1,2).

The psalmist wrote, "God is our refuge and strength, a very present help in trouble. Therefore will not we fear, though the earth be removed, and though the mountains be carried into the midst of the sea; though the waters thereof roar and be troubled, though the mountains shake with the swelling thereof" (Psalm 46:1-3).

God said to his people, "I have loved you with an everlasting love; I have drawn you with loving-kindness" (Jeremiah 31:3).

Through Isaiah, Jehovah said, "I have not spoken in

secret, in a dark place of the earth: I said not unto the seed of Jacob, Seek ye me in vain: I the Lord speak righteousness, I declare things that are right" (Isaiah 45:19).

God is present because he is love (1 John 4:12). Shakespeare was right when he observed, "They do not love that do not show their love." Love is, above all, the gift of oneself. When one loves, he cherishes the beloved, forming a union with someone outside himself. A God of love cannot make himself known except by love. That God from the beginning has been present among his people is not, therefore, surprising.

> *We occupy ourselves with the endless, meaningless, unanticipated demands of church life, and the necessary activities of spiritual development go neglected. We are too busy to pursue God, who, alone, can satisfy the longing of the human heart.*

We should emphasize the Lord's presence more than his promised second coming. After all, it is with the Presence that we now have to deal. The Lord is here, whatever we may think about it or feel about it. If we were more aware of God's presence, our sorrow would turn into joy, our weakness into strength, and our night into day. Greater awareness of God's presence also would cure worry, bring peace, and restore our sense of mission.

If you ache for God, you will delight in the following chapters of this book. If, like David, you want to follow hard after God (Psalm 63:8), and if, like David, you want to "taste and see" the Lord (Psalm 34:8), then you will rejoice as you proceed with a reading of the following pages. As for the rest, I pray that something will incite a flame of passion for the living God.

Questions for Discussion

1. Why is Arthur Schopenhauer incorrect in his conclusion that the world "is something which ought not to be"?

2. What is life's purpose? Is life worth living?
3. Is God dead? How do you know?
4. Is it possible for God to be alive, but dead for those who believe in him? Explain.
5. What is meant by the phrase, "activity without insight"?
6. Why is "activity without insight" one of the common mistakes of believers?
7. What is the real danger of "activity without insight"?
8. Why does God choose to be present among his people?
9. If God is always with us, why does he seem distant and unreal?
10. How can you become more aware of God?

---

1. Clarence Darrow, "Is Life Worth Living?", pamphlet, (Girard, Kansas, no publisher) p. 43)

2. Leo Tolstoy, *A Confession, The Gospel in Brief and What I Believe,* translated by Aylmer Maude, (London, 1940).

3. Arthur Schopenhauer, *The World as Will and Idea,* translated by R. B. Haldane and J. Kemp, 1883, (Lawrence, Kansas, AMS Pub.) vol. 3, p. 390.

CHAPTER 2

A Sense of Absence

A dear friend of mine was born blind. He confessed to me once that he doesn't find it disturbing when others speak about the beauties of nature or the marvelous blessing of sight. He explained that he had never experienced the sensation of sight and, therefore, had no sense of its absence.

Because having a sense of absence without having a sense of presence is difficult, I was unaware of the poverty of my childhood. My early childhood was spent in the rural South. My parents were honest and hard-working, but poor. Like most in our community, we grew large vegetable gardens that supplied more than enough food during the growing season. Food not eaten during the summer months was canned and stored in reserve for winter.

We purchased flour, sugar and potatoes at the local farmer's market. I recall that some brands of flour came packaged in 50- and 100-pound cloth sacks that people prized because the patterns made the material suitable for sewing. To see a brother and a sister going to school with matching shirt and blouse was common.

Every fall, just before school began, I got one pair of shoes that had to last all year. I had few clothes, no allowance, and no stereo or television; I never went to McDonald's.

We were poor! At the time, however, I did not resent being poor. I know now that I was poor, but I did not know it at the time. I had no sense of the absence of money simply because I had no sense of presence of material wealth.

Absence Without Presence?

Owing to my conviction that it is difficult to have a sense of absence without a sense of presence, I wonder if the atheist isn't more aware of God than he wants to confess. I wonder if the atheist who militantly announces, "God does not exist," is fully aware of the implications of his conclusion. Without a sense of Divine Presence, it is difficult to achieve a sense of absence.

Absence Among Believers

What worries me, however, is the genuine sense of absence among many believers. It isn't that these Christians flatly deny God's existence; rather, they perceive God as impersonal and remote. God lives in their thoughts but not in their hearts. The loss of any sense of a living experience of God is clear. The precious church of Christ as a whole is in a period of spiritual deprivation and impoverishment while totally unaware of

> *If God is to become real to us, we must take refuge from our secular thoughts and let our burdens and distractions wait. We must "take time to be holy."*

its poverty. The church has little sense of Divine absence because it has had little sense of Divine Presence.

Development of a sense of Presence is the most important activity of the believer's life. Without a sense of Presence, one is never safe from the ravages of sin. All my life I have heard that our only refuge from sin is to have a passionate hatred for wickedness. The problem with that concept is that humanity, weak and frail, has never learned to hate sin enough. Actually, our only security from sin and its consequences is to love God above all.

David's Sense of Presence

King David, more than anyone, illustrates the importance of a well-developed sense of Presence. In spite of his incomparable virtues, David committed some of the blackest sins recorded in the Bible. For all his strengths, David also had weaknesses. David was a fierce warrior, but he also could cringe like a baby. David was a strong and able administrator, yet he often was helpless before the resourceful Joab who maneuvered him into many dilemmas.

David's lust, immorality and murder reveal human sin in its ugliest forms. Hypocrisy can be added to the list of his sins because David made an effort to appear casual when the news reached him about the death of Uriah, the husband of Bathsheba. He said to the messenger, "Don't let this upset you; the sword devours one as well as another" (2 Samuel 11:25). In effect, David tried to pass off the whole episode of Uriah's death with the flippant comment, "Death is no respector of persons."

Although David tried to appear casual, his spirit churned in agony. In Psalm 32:3,4, David reflects on his misery during his period of unforgiven sin: "When I kept silent, my bones wasted away through my groaning all day long. For day and night your hand was heavy upon me; my strength was sapped as in the heat of summer."

David committed unspeakable sins and went so far away from God that it is a wonder he found it possible to repent. What brought David back to God? Only his sense of Presence. David loved God deeply and, therefore, could not live with the thought of separation from him. David's deep sense of Presence is seen in Psalm 139:1-12:

> O Lord, you have searched me
>   and you know me.
> You know when I sit and when I rise;
>   you perceive my thoughts from afar.
> You discern my going out and my lying down;
>   you are familiar with all my ways.
> Before a word is on my tongue
>   you know it completely, O Lord.

You hem me in, behind and before;
    you have laid your hand upon me.
Such knowledge is too wonderful for me,
    too lofty for me to attain.

Where can I go from your Spirit?
    Where can I flee from your presence?
If I go up to the heavens, you are there;
    if I make my bed in the depths, you are there.
If I rise on the wings of the dawn,
    if I settle on the far side of the sea,
even there your hand will guide me,
    your right hand will hold me fast.

If I say, "Surely the darkness will hide me
    and the light become night around me,"
even the darkness will not be dark to you;
    the night will shine like the day,
    for the darkness is as light to you.

David's Sense of Absence

When David fell, the one thing that bothered him most was a sense of Divine absence. In his repentance David prayed, "Do not cast me from your presence or take your Holy Spirit from me" (Psalm 51:11). David's salvation from the terrible consequences of his sin may be attributed to his inability to live without God. David was forgiven for much because he loved much.

Only in a deep sense of Presence can we ever have a sense of absence. When sin overcomes us, our only hope of recovery is the precious memory of sweet fellowship with God. We never find our way out of sin because of a hatred for wickedness, but if we love God above all, we must find our way back to him or our hearts burst.

Again, however, I worry about the genuine sense of absence among God's children. God isn't real in the experience of most Christians, and sadly, they are totally unaware of their spiritual poverty. They feel no sense of absence because there was never a sense of Presence.

13

How did this generation of Christians lose awareness of the presence of God?

Ambition with Blindness

One reason most modern Christians have lost a sense of Presence is that they are too busy building churches to pursue God. Unlike the early church, characterized by informal worship, simple organizational structure, and an emphasis upon the individual and his personal relationship with God, the modern church often measures success in corporate advertisements, huge corporate programs with massive budgets and complicated administrative machinery.

A tendency exists to desire glory for the church rather than for God. We want to tell the world how large and influential the church is rather than speak of how glorious God is as revealed in Christ. More concern is expressed about advertising the church than telling about Christ who is the head of the church.

With our pride in costly buildings, massive budgets, administrative machinery, giant business, desirable locations and influential people, our egos swell. This partially explains the reason for the ridiculous spirit of competition that exists among churches. We feel compelled to build the most impressive church around because we substitute ourselves for the Lord. Subconsciously

> *We never find our way out of sin because of a hatred for wickedness, but if we love God above all, we must find our way back to him or our hearts burst.*

we want the praise of men when we boast of the corporate achievements of the church. I easily can root for "my church" because I identify with it and I will receive reflected credit if the church does well. We forget that the scriptures do not tell us to seek glory for the church, but to glorify God in the church (Ephesians 3:20,21).

A climate that obscures a sense of Presence often exists in the church. Because of our emphasis on outward show, sound preaching that helps the Christian build his relationship with God has little place. In an atmosphere where the success of the church depends on corporate achievements, pulpit responsibilities often are left to less thoughtful men. It becomes unnecessary for the shepherd to point his sheep toward God, so long as he is extroverted, talkative and dynamic and can "sell the program." Absence of fire is inconsequential. A flash of neon is everything. Sadly, the sheep are unaware that the difference between a neon shepherd and a shepherd with the fire of Divine Presence is the difference between thunder and lightning. One is ostentatious, but benign. The other is an awesome manifestation of power.

True worship is all but lost in many churches. The hungry sheep congregate at the Lord's table to feed on a steady diet that succeeds only in oiling the machines that run the programs. One of the great scandals of the modern church is that the sheep enter the fold to see their Guide and are sent away satisfied, although they never saw their Lord. The flock is spiritually impoverished and yet unaware of its poverty. They feel no sense of absence because there was never a sense of Presence.

The Feverish Gait

Another obstacle to the development of a sense of Presence is the demanding world in which we live. If we spend 15 hours and 55 minutes each day thinking about the temporal affairs of the world and spend only the remaining five minutes of our waking time reflecting on spiritual matters, then inevitably God will seem unreal to us. If God is to become real to us, we must take refuge from our secular thoughts and let our burdens and distractions wait. We must "take time to be holy."

Life is filled with unanticipated demands. If we are not careful, thoughts of God escape us entirely. Meister Eckhart, a 13th century German theologian and philosopher, wrote: "No man ever wanted anything so much as God wants to make the soul aware of him. God is ever ready, but we are unready. God is in, we are out; God is home, we are strangers."

15

If God is to be known in personal experience, we must lift up our eyes of faith daily. It takes practice to see the things that are invisible to the natural eye.

The Remote God

Many people never develop a sense of Presence because they convince themselves that God is distant and, therefore, difficult to find. If we seek for God as if he were far removed from us and locked behind walls and gates of pearl, it will be impossible to become aware of his presence. Only when we understand that no space is free of him can we find God in everything and everywhere.

We make a mistake in thinking that God must be "found." God is intimately present. The need is not to find God but to become aware of him. Gerald Massey wrote:

Eternity is not beyond the stars—
Some far Hereafter—it is Here, and Now!
We do not see it save by spirit-sight.
We shut our eyes in prayer, and we are
     There
In thought, and Thoughts are spirit-things—
Realities upon the other side.

Those who roam to distant places in search of a God who is near are like the individual who looked for his lost pen. He looked diligently in every room and searched every drawer only to discover that the pen was in his pocket near his heart all the while. Thomas Edward Brown wrote it this way:

Expecting Him, my door was open wide;
     Then I looked round
If any lack of service might be found,
And saw Him at my side:
How entered, by what secret stair,
I know not, knowing only He was there.

God is always near and never difficult to find. All that remains is for us to grow in our sense of Presence. We must never allow our religion to satisfy itself with anything less than God. We must constantly look for God's face and listen for his voice. Never take refuge in a superficial religion.

Questions for Discussion

1. "There can be no sense of absence without a sense of presence." Explain.
2. Do you feel that the militant atheist is more aware of God than he knows or is willing to admit? Why?
3. Why is it important to have a sense of Presence?
4. What brought David to repentance—his hatred of sin or his need for fellowship with God?
5. How is it possible for God's people to be spiritually impoverished and have no knowledge of their poverty?
6. How does building churches and administering programs crowd God out of our lives?
7. Are we to seek glory for the church or for God? Is there a difference?
8. How is God glorified in the church?
9. In a busy world, how does one find time to pursue God?
10. In what ways can the Christian religion become superficial?

CHAPTER 3

A Sense of Presence

Poets often speak of the well-developed sense of Presence among children. Robert Browning wrote:

> The Child
> Feels God a moment, ichors [scars] o'er the place
> Plays on and grows to be a man like us.

Browning's point is that children, aware of God in the beginning, manage to harden their sensitivity to Divine Presence and finally grow up to be "like us"—adults without a sense of Presence.

Unquestionably, children have a profound sense of God's presence. This was exemplified when my daughter, Cindy, and my grandchildren Kristen and Shaun spent six weeks at our house while Jonn, my son-in-law, made preparations for his family to begin a new life in Houston. Early the first day of his visit, Shaun announced his intention to "sleep with Haw Paw in Haw Paw's bed." (My name is "Paw Paw," but Shaun couldn't pronounce two words together which begin with the letter "P.") Every night for six weeks, Shaun fell to sleep in my arms.

A typical night began with Shaun saying, "Haw Paw, I want you to hold me." I now know how right Euripides was when he said, "How delicate the skin, how sweet the breath of children." While in my embrace, our faces an inch apart, Shaun breathed his nightly prayer:

> Now I lay me down to sleep;
>   I pray the Lord my soul to keep;
> If I should die before I wake,

18

I pray the Lord my soul to take.
In Jesus' name, Amen.

After the prayer was concluded, conversation always turned to the subject of God. Shaun was full of questions. One night he asked, "Where is God's bed?" I answered his difficult question as best I could. Shaun then confided that he had seen God awake at Bible class. "If I get afraid tonight," he said, "God will wake up." I was about to make the point that God always watches over us and that we should love him more than anyone when Shaun interrupted, "Haw Paw, I got to hoo poo, but when I got back from the bathroom, I want to still talk about God." Upon his return, with profound wisdom for anyone, to say nothing of a 4-year-old, Shaun confessed, "Haw Paw, I love God, and I love every peoples."

I marvel at a child's sense of Presence. Children know that God watches over them, even when they sleep. When morning comes they often pray the second part of Eugene Henry Pullen's touching prayer:

Now I wake and see the light;
'Tis God who kept me through the night.
To Him I lift my voice and pray
That He will keep me through the day.
In Jesus' name, Amen.

I read about an incident in the life of Helen Keller that forcefully illustrates a child's sensitivity to God. Helen spent her childhood behind an impervious veil of blindness and a barricade of deafness. She found a bright and bustling world through the vocabulary of touch. Phillips Brooks allowed Helen to place her fingers on his lips as he talked in simple language about God and the disclosure of himself in the person of his son Jesus Christ. While listening with her fingers, Helen grew fidgety. Abruptly she cried out, "I knew him! I knew him! I didn't know his name, but I knew him!"

Lost Sensitivity

The sad thing is that the child who "feels God for a

moment," to quote Browning, often "ichors [scars] o'er the place" and loses his sensitivity for the remainder of life.

When I moved 20 years ago to the church I still serve, I met a little boy who was very sensitive to God. Wonder and awe filled his heart as he attended Bible classes to hear about Jesus. That boy, so aware of God, is now a university student.

I recently made a speech for a group of students at that university in which I affirmed my belief in God. My friend, who as a child had a profound sense of Presence, approached to offer his opinion that my faith in God was only the consequence of what my parents, kindred and teachers had conditioned me to accept. "A person of your intelligence," he said, "would not believe in the existence of God if you had not been raised by believing parents and taught by Christian teachers."

My young friend is now a skeptic who fails to recognize that philosophy can do nothing that faith cannot do better. I cannot get through to him that faith can do a great many things that philosophy cannot do at all. Philosophy boasts that it gives new understanding, but only faith can give new insight. Philosophy boasts of new avenues, but only faith can give us strength to stroll the old ones. Philosophy boasts of new responsibilities, but only faith can instill courage to fulfill the old obligations that are plain before us. Philosophy cannot satisfy the longings of the immortal soul, for the heart was made for God and only faith can fill it.

In the process of growing up, a bright young man has managed to scar over his area of sensitivity to God, and now he thinks that a person of my intelligence would not believe in the existence of God if I had not been reared by believing parents and taught by Christian teachers. He no longer can accept God's reality because he takes great pride in being intellectual. Somewhere along the way he bought the silly notion that intelligence precludes faith. He seems unaware that many eminent scientists, scholars and even philosophers have had no problem in accepting God's reality. Fénelon, Bossuet, Racine, Newton and Pascal—some of the most enlightened men of history—not only believed God exists, but accepted the divinity of Jesus Christ as well.

My young friend now believes that faith and reason cannot dwell together in the same heart. He believes that faith contradicts reason and reason rejects faith. When will he learn that intellect without faith makes one no better than the animal who lives a visionless life within his brain? Soon, I pray.

Emotion and Reason

The supposed hostility between emotion and reason is an old debate. Some advise us to govern ourselves by reason and not to let emotions run wild. Others tell us that life without emotion remains cold and unappealing. Which is it to be? Are we to give our emotions free course or hold them in check? Is reason to reign supreme, or should we throw caution to the wind?

Even within religious circles, some people think emotion and reason are incompatible. I believe that both reason and emotion are parts of man's nature and are, therefore, necessary components of moral virtue and action. Granted, emotion must be properly subordinated to reason, but emotion is what always motivates one to act on

> *The heart was made for God and only faith can fill it.*

the knowledge he gains. Reason can no more influence the will and operate as a motive than the eyes one uses to find his way can enable him to move from one place to another. The soundest reason will produce no more conviction in an empty heart than the most superficial argument. Both an anvil and a feather fall with equal velocity in a vacuum. Reason is our compass, but emotions are the winds that drive our sails.

Only a childlike emotional response to God will make it possible for us to develop and maintain a sense of Presence. As children, we all have a tender place for God. We do not have to "scar" our sensitive area over as we grow older.

21

The Example of David

The psalmist, for example, never lost his awareness of Presence. David was not only intelligent, but he lived in a real world with the kind of problems that might make one forget spiritual pursuits entirely. He was not sensitive to God's presence because he was a contemplative man with a lot of time on his hands. True, David was aesthetically sensitive, but he was also a brave guerrilla leader. If David was a singer of songs, musician, and poet with a genius for religion, he was also an astute diplomat, warrior king, consummate politician, and a man driven by erotic passion.

David never, however, became insensitive to God. In Psalm 18, a Psalm of thanksgiving, David wrote this:

I love you, O Lord, my strength.
The Lord is my rock, my fortress and my
　deliverer;
　my God is my rock, in whom I take refuge.
He is my shield and the horn of my salvation,
　my stronghold.
I call to the Lord, who is worthy of praise,
　and I am saved from my enemies.

(v. 1-3)

Presence and Power

The journey from a shepherd's hut to the king's palace was treacherous. All along the way God's hovering presence preceded David in battle. Except for Divine nearness, David would have died a thousand deaths.

He reached down from on high and took hold
　of me;
　he drew me out of deep waters.
He rescued me from my powerful enemy,
　from my foes, who were too strong for me.
They confronted me in the day of my disaster,
　but the Lord was my support.

(Psalm 18:16-19)

22

Presence and Praise

When David considered Divine Presence, how God always stood by him, he shouted:

For who is God besides the Lord?
And who is the Rock except our God?
It is God who arms me with strength
and makes my way perfect.
He makes my feet like the feet of a deer;
he enables me to stand on the heights.
He trains my hands for battle;
my arms can bend a bow of bronze.
You give me your shield of victory,
and your right hand sustains me;
you stoop down to make me great.
(Psalm 18:31-35)

Presence and Conscience

David not only conquered the enemies without, but through a sense of Presence, he also conquered the enemy within. After the incident with Bathsheba, the psalmist prayed this prayer:

Do not cast me from your presence
or take your Holy Spirit from me.
Restore to me the joy of your salvation
and grant me a willing spirit, to sustain me.

Then I will teach transgressors your ways,
and sinners will turn back to you.
(Psalm 51:11-13)

God's presence sharpened the psalmist's conscience and activated his will to avoid evil. David's sense of Presence stirred him to new heights of spirituality that empowered him to conquer the enemy of passion.

No man is good enough, strong enough or wise enough to solve his physical and spiritual problems. Man is a creature, and in crisis situations such as war, sickness, sin and death, man either must have a sense of Presence or remain without strength to endure.

Sensitive to Presence

Nowhere is it written that the child must grow up to lose his sense of Presence. We do not have to let the qualities of childhood, such as inquisitiveness, alertness and sensitivity, to fade into the past.

Reason is our compass, but emotions are the winds that drive our sails.

A sense of Presence is still possible. I encourage each reader to become alert to God's nearness. God is present even though we may be unaware of it, but, like David's, our lives would be so much more heroic if we had a sharp sense of Presence.

Questions for Discussion

1. What are the qualities in children that make them aware of God's presence?
2. Do most believers have faith in God only because they were raised by believing parents? What is your proof?
3. Is there danger in inherited faith? If so, what is the danger? Why?
4. Does a conflict exist between reason and faith? What is the conflict?
5. How did David's sense of Presence make it possible for him to overpower his enemies without? His passion within?
6. How does one develop a sense of God's presence?
7. Why are believers often unaware of God's presence?
8. Can one live in a busy world and successfully pursue a sense of Presence? Why not or how?
9. What is the role of emotion in religious experience?
10. What is the role of intellect in religious experience?

CHAPTER 4

Longing for God

Blaise Pascal was a great mathematician during a time when the area of mathematics was studied extensively. He founded the modern theory of probabilities, invented the mathematical triangle (Pascal's triangle), discovered the properties of the cycloid, and contributed to the advancement of differential calculus. In physics his experiments increased knowledge of atmospheric pressure through barometric measurements and of the equilibrium of fluids.

Pascal's Law states that "pressure applied to a confined fluid at any point is transmitted undiminished through the fluid in all directions and acts upon every part of the confining vessel at right angles to its interior surfaces and equally upon equal areas." Practical applications of Pascal's Law are seen in the countless hydraulic systems that make it possible for us to brake our cars, fly in airplanes, and do other incredible tasks.

After his death, Pascal's family discovered a piece of parchment sewed into his doublet (a close-fitting body-garment worn by men from the 14th to the 18th centuries). On the parchment was a crude sketch of the cross and some phrases that revealed Pascal's longing for God. Trying to describe the indescribable joy of Presence, he exclaimed, "From half-past ten till half-past twelve, Fire!" Pascal shouts in astonishment, "Not the God of philosophers and of scholars! . . . Certitude! Certitude! Joy! Peace! . . . The world has not known Thee, but I have known Thee . . . Joy! Joy! Joy! Abundance of Joy!"

Although a great scientist, Pascal thought reason could not solve man's problems or satisfy his hopes. He exalted a sense of Presence as our only means of fulfillment, saying, "The heart has its reasons which reason itself knows nothing of."

A sense of Presence was so important to Pascal that when he felt the fire beginning to die he cried, "Are you departing from me? Oh, let me not be separated from You eternally!"

Love and Presence

The human spirit always cries out for the presence of those it loves. The year I left home, I recall my dad saying, "Son, remember that letters have no arms." Dad was not discouraging the writing of letters; he appreciated letters. However, a time comes when nothing but the embrace of those we love can satisfy the yearning breast.

Having children of my own, I have learned that the desire to embrace loved ones can be irresistible. I have three children and two grandchildren. My family has always been close-knit and loving. Until recently, none of us lived more than a few miles apart, which is unusual considering I am the pulpit minister for a local church, an occupation that, seems never to leave one in the same location for extended periods of time. As it turns out, however, I have served one church for 20 years.

While living in the same house on Rovey Street in Phoenix, my children received their education, grew to adulthood, married, and began their own families. Our geographical closeness made it possible for us to visit often. What joy we knew in one another's presence!

Then came the day when Cindy, my oldest daughter, announced that new job responsibilities for her husband Jonn made it necessary for them to move to a distant state. No longer is it possible to visit my grandchildren any time the idea comes to mind.

Though a great distance separates me from my loved ones, I do not doubt their existence. Nor do I doubt they love me as I love them. I am somewhat consoled by the telephone, which makes it possible for me to talk with the children any time I ache to hear from them. Sometimes, however, merely talking long-distance isn't enough. Although I feel joy upon hearing the garbled, unintelligible syllables of a 1-year-old granddaughter and "I love you, Haw Paw," from a 4-year-old grandson, at times my soul longs for their presence. When my heart is hungry for the children's presence, nothing will do but for me to take a few days off, schedule a flight with one of the airlines, and go to behold those I love. Telephones have no arms, either.

But What About God?

If we love God with all our heart, soul, mind, and strength, then at times the longing for Presence is so intense that only a God with arms can satisfy the passion within.

My spirit therefore rejoices in the knowledge that God has an "outstretched arm" that always remains extended toward his loving children. Some will argue that God's "outstretched arm" is merely an anthropomorphic term, not to be taken literally. Even if I grant, however, that the "outstretched arm" of God is an anthropomorphism, requiring metaphorical interpretation, what is the meaning of the metaphor? Is it not that God is powerful to embrace, protect and love those who long for Presence?

In Luke 15, Jesus told an unforgettable story that beautifully illustrates the seeking, searching, missionary heart of God. The story describes to us a God with open arms to receive, at any moment, those who seek his Presence.

According to the Lord's story, an old man had two sons. The younger son came to his father one day, asking for his share of family wealth. The young man then went to a foreign country where he wasted everything in sinful living. Destitute and without friends, the young man took a job feeding hogs, a demeaning job for a young Jew who considered swine ceremonially unclean.

One day, he "came to himself" and decided to return home to his father. He said, "I will arise and go to my father, and will say unto him, Father, I have sinned against heaven, and before thee, and am no more worthy to be called thy son: make me as one of thy hired servants" (Luke 15:18,19).

Before the young man got all the way home, when "he was yet a great way off, his father saw him, and had compassion, and ran, and fell on his neck, and kissed him. . . . The father said to his servants, Bring forth the best robe, and put it on him; and put a ring on his hand, and shoes on his feet: And bring hither the fatted calf, and kill it; and let us eat, and be merry: For my son was dead, and is alive again; he was lost, and is found . . ." (Luke 15:20,22-24).

Have you ever asked how, on the particular day the prodigal returned home, his father happened to see him coming down the road? How long was the prodigal son gone from home? I suspect he was gone quite a while—long enough, at least, to spend all his money and eventually realize his mistake. How is it, then, that after the passing of months, perhaps years, the father met his son on the road the one day he chose to return? I believe a father's love watched that road every day, looking—longing—to embrace a wayward son.

> *One of the great lessons learned from Jesus' choice of the Twelve is that God seeks intimacy with us all, without regard to our social, political or economic differences.*

Have you noticed that the old man is the one who recognized his son at a great distance (Luke 15:20)? Have you also noticed, according to the same verse, that it is the old man who "ran" to his son? Usually, the eyes of the old are weak and their limbs and lungs are incapable of wind sprints.

In Jesus' story we learn that God longingly watches for us to make the first move toward him. Grace then puts wings on the Father's feet as he speeds out to embrace us, kiss us, and give us his best blessings.

Anyone who reads the Scriptures becomes aware that God is so eager to embrace us that he has sometimes shown up uninvited. Moses preferred to be left alone when God called to him from a burning bush and gave him a commission to lead Israel. For 40 years Moses had been a shepherd. He had job security. Everything was peaceful. No matter how much he sympathized with his enslaved Hebrew brethren, Moses did not want to leave the tranquillity of home. Uninvited and unwelcome, God approached Moses with a bold plan to deliver his people from slavery.

Why would God approach a man who preferred to be left alone? I believe that God not only wanted Moses for a job, but he also longed for Moses' companionship. Moses is the one with whom the Lord spoke "face to face, as a man speaks with his friend" (Exodus 33:11).

Jesus

In a similar way, Jesus called the 12 apostles, not only because he needed preachers, evangelists and apostles, but because he needed their companionship. Jesus chose them "that they should be with him . . ." (Mark 3:14).

The phrase, "that they should be with him," implies intimacy. That Jesus sought companionship does not surprise me. What does startle me a little is that he sought the friendship of men who were so diverse that one wonders how they ever managed to come together in a common cause. Peter and John, for example, could not be more different. Peter was bold and impulsive, and John was quiet, thoughtful and loving. Most of the disciples were believing, but Thomas seemed always incredulous, playing the role of a skeptic. The political differences between Matthew and Simon the Canaanite were so potentially explosive one wonders how they ever avoided being at each other's throats. Matthew was a tax collector and servant of the Roman governor, and Simon was a zealot and rebel against Rome. He would have hated Rome and taxes and those who gathered them.

One of the great lessons learned from Jesus' choice of the Twelve is that God seeks intimacy with us all, without regard to our social, political or economic differences.

Some will ask, "Why should God desire our companionship? What can we do for God?" My answer is that I believe God wants the comfort of our love, which explains why Jesus wanted Peter, James and John with him when he faced the ordeal of Gethsemane. Jesus needed friendly hands and voices. Instead, he found three sleeping disciples. Jesus asked, "Could ye not watch with me one hour?" Our Lord's wistful question reveals a heart crying out for human support and sympathy.

Jesus longed for the companionship of men who would be faithful friends, no matter what happened. The disciples often disappointed Jesus, but he knew they ultimately would prove their friendship. With appreciation, Jesus, the night before he died, said to his disciples in the upper room, "You are those who have stood by me in my trials" (Luke 22:28).

Jesus portrays to us a God who seeks intimacy with humans. If God does not desire intimacy, how are we to explain Jesus' teaching about the vine and branches, Paul's declaration that the church is Christ's bride, or James' promise, "Draw nigh to God, and he will draw nigh to you" (James 4:8)?

God Is Approachable

I can get as near to God as my heart desires. Unlike the great and mighty of earth, God does not live a guarded life behind high walls. He does not cloister himself in the throne room. No secretaries will deny me an interview. Men cannot keep me from God unless I let them. Satan may fight me all the way, but not even the powers of darkness can deny me the pleasure of God's company.

God-hungry people find God. The empty God stalker is filled, never to hunger or thirst again. Those with a lust for God find their spiritual nakedness clothed with the blessed Presence.

If you think I am encouraging what some call "over-spirituality" among God's people, I can only say that in "that great day," you will wear the name "over-spiritual" with pride.

The only safe course is to thirst after, long for, reach out, and cry aloud for God. Let your hunger and thirst for righteousness feed upon themselves. Refuse satisfaction, for when you think you know God well enough, you know him not at all. You can no more find out all there is to know about God than you can discover all there is to know about truth, beauty or eternity. If you long for God, however, you can learn enough about him to live nobly, courageously and joyfully.

Questions for Discussion

1. What did Pascal mean when he said, "The heart has its reasons which reason itself knows nothing of"?
2. Why do we long for the physical presence of those we love?
3. What was Jesus' purpose in telling the story of the prodigal son?
4. How do we know God longs for us?
5. What is meant by the statement, "God talked to Moses face to face"?
6. Why did Jesus call the Twelve?
7. Why does God want our companionship?
8. In what sense is the church the bride of Christ?
9. Is God approachable? How do you know?
10. How does one draw near to God?

CHAPTER 5

Loving God Above All

When one of the scribes asked Jesus what was the most important commandment of all, he answered, "Hear, O Israel; the Lord our God is one Lord: And thou shalt love the Lord thy God with all thy heart, and with all thy soul, and with all thy mind, and with all thy strength: this is the first commandment. And the second is like, namely this, Thou shalt love thy neighbor as thyself. There is none other commandment greater than these" (Mark 12:29-31).

I have noticed that obeying the second most important command—loving neighbors—is easier than obeying the most important command—loving God. The reason for this phenomenon is not difficult to understand. We can see our neighbors, but God is invisible, at least to the natural eye.

For a similar reason, many find it difficult to pray. One of the common complaints about prayer is, "It feels as if I'm talking to nothing."

The natural senses must always have difficulty seeing God, for God is "wholly other" than the physical world he made. The Old Testament emphasized the transcendence of God by the prohibition of idols. In a time when many worshiped graven images, Isaiah asked, "To whom, then, will you compare God? What image will you compare him to?" (Isaiah 40:18). The prophet answers, "Do you not know? Have you not heard? The Lord is the everlasting God, the Creator of the ends of the earth. He will not grow tired or weary, and his understanding no one can fathom (Isaiah 40:28).

The New Testament affirms that no one has ever seen God (John 1:18). The apostle Paul said that our perception of God is like a fuzzy reflection in a mirror: "Now we see but a poor reflection; then we shall see face to face. Now I know in part; then I shall know fully, even as I am fully known" (1 Corinthians 13:12). In his first letter to Timothy, the apostle said that God is immortal, dwelling in "unapproachable light, whom no one has seen or can see. To him be honor and might forever. Amen" (1 Timothy 6:16).

How are we to solve the problem created for us by the command to love an invisible God? For one thing, I do not believe that the object of love must always be visible to the physical eye. Every day of our lives we love things we do not see. For example, with the physical eye we cannot see the wisdom, sincerity or virtue of our friends, but we love these qualities and prefer them in those we know over wealth or outward beauty.

> *There is something special about the love between old people. I am impressed that the fading of physical beauty only serves to deepen true love.*

I have a friend who was born physically deformed. His blind, twisted and palsied body causes one, at first glance, to look away. He is also one of the most sensitive, intelligent and sincere Christians I have ever known. His sound common sense, kindness, and genuine Christian goodness make him, of all people I know, the easiest to love. I love him, not because he is one of the "beautiful people," but because his invisible qualities of faith and sincerity have won my devotion and respect.

A great truth is: "Love looks not with the eyes, but with the mind." Love that has nothing except what may be seen with the eyes to keep it in good health is short-lived. If others love you for your physical appeal, you are not genuinely loved. Age eventually will make your physical beauty fade. What then? What if some tragic accident left you disfigured and unsightly? Would you still be you? Would others still love you? You would, of course, still be you, and those whose love for you is sincere would not change their feelings toward you, for genuine love sees not with the eyes, but with the soul. Love does not ask for perfection in the object of its affection. It asks only for the privilege of receiving and caring.

For years I have jogged on the quiet streets of the Phoenix neighborhood where I live. During my jogging sessions, I often meet an elderly neighborhood couple taking their daily walk. With their hands clasped, and smiles on their faces, they greet everyone they see. The only unusual thing about the couple is that the old man carries a small baseball bat in his left hand. He carries the bat to protect his wife. She is somewhat feeble, and he fears that a neighborhood dog, either by attack or over-friendliness, might cause her injury. The old man's explanation for carrying a baseball bat is amusing, considering there are no loose pets in the neighborhood. Love is protective, however, and as I look at the old couple— stooped, wrinkled, walking hand-in-hand, and comforting and loving each other—I am impressed that there is something special about the love between old people. I am impressed that the fading of physical beauty only serves to deepen true love.

Because love sees with the heart, it never takes account of imperfections. Love hides a scar when it cannot be taken away and is never so blind as when it sees faults. Love is noble because it covers blemishes and excuses failings. Love hides weaknesses in silence and proclaims virtues upon the rooftop. Again, love sees with the soul, not with the eyes.

The Soul Sees God

The Bible affirms that although God is invisible to the natural eye, he is visible to the inward eye of faith. As the eye of faith focuses upon God and as obedience becomes the goal of the believer's heart, God takes shape. The point is powerfully made in John 14:21-23:

"He that hath my commandments, and keepeth them, he it is that loveth me: and he that loveth me shall be loved of my Father, and I will love him and will manifest myself to him. Judas saith unto him, not Iscariot, Lord, how is it that thou will manifest thyself unto us, and not unto the world? Jesus answered and said unto him, If a man love me, he will keep my words: and my Father will love him, and we will come unto him, and make our abode with him."

For those who have trained their inner eyes to see spiritual things, God becomes obvious. David said, "Taste and see that the Lord is good . . ." (Psalm 34:8). Jesus said, "My sheep listen to my voice" (John 10:27).

God is not vague to his people. He is always living, speaking and manifesting himself to those who have trained their spiritual senses to see and hear the Divine. Otherwise, how could the psalmist say this?

God is our refuge and strength, a very present help in trouble. Therefore will not we fear, though the earth be removed, and though the mountains be carried into the midst of the sea; Though the waters thereof roar and be troubled, though the mountains shake with the welling thereof . . . Be still, and know that I am God: I will be exalted among the heathen, I will be exalted in the earth. The Lord of hosts is with us; the God of Jacob is our refuge (Psalm 46:1-3,10,11).

God Dwells Within

In his first letter to the Corinthian church, Paul asked, "Know ye not that ye are the temple of God, and that the Spirit of God dwelleth in you" (1 Corinthians 3:16)? In the second letter to the Corinthians, the apostle further develops his thinking: "And what agreement hath the temple of God with idols? for ye are the temple of the living God; as God hath said, I will dwell in them, and walk in them; and I will be their God, and they shall be my people" (2 Corinthians 6:16).

The Presence is now in believers as living temples. The ancient Jewish temple was once God's dwelling place, but now God's habitation is the church.

The tabernacle and temple of the Old Testament were not only God's abiding places, but they were also his visible manifestations to Israel. Everything about the tabernacle and temple represented Presence and glory. In them, God, in awesome and glorious manifestation, presented himself to Israel.

Now, however, the believer is a living temple for Presence. Writing to Gentile Christians, Paul put it like this:

> Now therefore ye are no more strangers and foreigners, but fellow-citizens with the saints, and of the household of God; And are built upon the foundation of the apostles and prophets, Jesus Christ himself being the chief corner stone; In whom all the building fitly framed together groweth unto a holy temple in the Lord: In whom ye also are builded together for a habitation of God through the Spirit (Ephesians 2:19-22).

The soul—the inner eye—sees God. How could it be otherwise, considering God dwells within? God may be invisible to natural sight, but spiritual sight always detects him.

Genuine love sees not with the eyes, but with the soul. Love does not ask for perfection in the object of its affection.

Because we know God spiritually—apart from all physical forms—we love him. We do not love him for the beauty of any visible thing like nature or the melodies we hear or the fragrance of the flowers, for all such things are mere works of God. We love God for himself.

When we love God himself, it becomes possible for us to meet all other obligations of the Christian life. Whether the command is to evangelize, love our neighbors, refrain from immorality, pray for our enemies, or to help the weak, we always find a way to obey if we love God with all our heart.

Our most important duty is not to attend church services or to be a good parent, spouse or soul-winner, though these are important. Our greatest charge is to love God with our whole beings. If we love God intensely, we always will find a way to serve the church, be good to our families, and win souls.

Love and Perception

Most important of all, nothing inspires a sense of Presence like passionate love for God. Precisely for this reason Jesus said love for God is the supreme command.

Genuine love is the irresistible desire to be in the presence of the one loved. Goethe correctly observed that "A life without love, without the presence of the beloved, is nothing but a mere magic-lantern show. We draw slide after slide, swiftly tiring of each, and pushing it back to make haste for the next." A lover is restless until he is in the presence of his beloved, and as John Dryden put it: "Love reckons hours for months, and days for years; And every little absence is an age."

When one loves God supremely, a sense of Divine absence is intolerable. Every moment away from Presence seems an eternity. An old German proverb says, "Love knows the hidden paths." Every lover of God finds a way to the object of his love, no matter how remote God may seem or how far the lover must travel.

Nothing quickens perception like love. I notice what my children wear because I love them. I am aware when they look depressed, happy or ill. Because I love my wife, I am able to close my eyes and recall a vivid picture of just how she looked when she left the house this morning. I remember the dress and the jewelry she wore. I can see the color of her hair, remember the scent of her perfume, and feel again the warmth and texture of her skin as we embraced and said goodbye for the day.

In a similar way, nothing arouses Divine perception like genuine love for God. Keenness of observation is born under the influence of a love for God that drives away the obscuring clouds of selfishness and sin.

Love God more, and you will become more aware of him. As you grow in your love for a God who loves you—as your respect deepens for a God who respects you—your sense of Presence will exceed the limits of human joy.

Questions for Discussion

1. What is the greatest command? Why?
2. Why is it difficult to love God above all?
3. What are some things in life we love but do not see?
4. Do you agree that love looks with the mind and not with the eyes? Explain.
5. Why does love not take account of imperfections?
6. How does the soul see God?
7. Is God vague to his people? Why?
8. Why does love increase perception of the one loved?
9. What is meant by the phrase, "Love knows the hidden paths"?
10. Why does a sense of Presence fill us with joy?

CHAPTER 6

Being and Seeing

When I first thought of including this chapter in the book you now read, I had a nagging thought in the back of my mind that said, "Edwin, here is an area where you would do well to remain silent." The temptation to omit it was powerful.

I have delivered countless sermons that warned of the dangers of speaking too quickly. I often say that silence is desirable because it never provokes envy or injures anyone's feelings. We seldom regret our silence, but we all deplore those thoughtless words that hurt others and strain relationships.

At this precise moment, however, I am in the grip of a quite different thought. It occurs to me that silence, like speech, also has the capacity to injure others. These lines I memorized as a child illustrate my point:

> Sticks and stones are hard on bones,
>   Aimed with angry art;
> Words can sting like anything,
>   But silence breaks the heart.

If prudence and kindness dictate silence in some circumstances, in others, prudence of a higher order may justify our speaking our thoughts. Within the family circle, for example, we always should voice our love. If someone attempts to destroy the character of another, we should speak a word in his defense.

Another consideration is the nature of life. Life is dynamic. Because of the nature of life, there can be no empty space or empty time. Therefore, silence is momentary and always must have its climax. "An absolute silence," said Jean Jacques Rousseau, an 18th century French philosopher, "leads to sadness: it is the image of death."

One thing more deserves some thought. Although silence may prevent me from being openly wrong, it always will deprive me of the possibility of being openly right. If my tongue remains in a closed mouth, how will anyone know whether I have a gem of truth? If I have a good reason to speak, I must speak.

What gem of truth do I have that requires such courage to communicate? Simply this: *"There is a connection between being and seeing."*

The connection between being and seeing was made by Jesus when he said, "Blessed are the pure in heart: for they shall see God" (Matthew 5:8).

God remains obscured to the present church age because its heart is yet impure. Mere external morality never comprehends God. If the heart is evil, it makes no difference how many times we wash our hands or clean the pots and pans. The Pharisees faithfully kept such rituals, but they never honored God with their hearts (Mark 7:3-13).

The Danger of Outward Forms

George Bungay expressed a common view when he wrote:

In rituals and faith excel!
Chimed out the Episcopalian bell.
All is well! is well! is well!
Pealed out the good old Dutch church bell.

All is not well, however, just because one excels in the external observance of the rituals and forms of religion. True religion intensely focuses on God and is always more inward than outward. After his sin with Bathsheba, David cried out for God and found him, not because of a sacrifice of burnt offering, but because he had a change of heart. David knew that the sacrifice God required was humility of spirit. He prayed: "For thou desirest not sacrifice; else would I give it: thou delightest not in burnt offering. The sacrifices of God are a broken spirit: a broken and contrite heart, O God, thou wilt not despise" (Psalm 51:16,17).

The danger of trusting the outward forms of religion was often on the apostle Paul's mind. When he wrote to the Galatian churches, he expressed a fear that he had bestowed upon them "labour in vain" because they observed "days, and months, and times, and years" (Galatians 4:10,11).

By painstaking observance of special religious feasts and rituals, Galatian Christians believed they had fully discharged their duty before God. Paul warned the Galatians that to make Christianity a religion of rituals was to make it a system of legalism, which did not remotely resemble the prophetic religion of Christ. Not only would outward forms—if relied upon as effectual in and of themselves—make the Galatians legalists, but would also keep them from seeing God. Paul is clear in his warning: "But now that you know God—or rather are known by God—how is it that you are turning back to those weak and miserable principles? Do you wish to be enslaved by them all over again?" (Galatians 4:9).

> *"Ritual" is not a dirty word. The problem is that we focus so much attention on our forms, customs and traditions, that we fail to see God.*

Imprisonment is always the result of too much trust in outward forms. Excessive love for ritual locks one in the darkest, innermost dungeon of spiritual blindness. The answer to the problem, however, is not to throw caution to the wind and declare freedom from all outward forms and traditions. To the contrary, a strong case can be made for the point that freedom without God-given rituals and traditions goes berserk. The solution is not to junk our forms, but to understand that we often allow them to become our jailers.

One widespread feeling, for example, is that we faithfully discharge our Christian duty when we meet on Sunday to participate in fellowship of the Lord's Supper. Many believe that faithful observance of the Supper is the one necessary activity that will guarantee continued spiritual life and acceptance of God. Poorly taught Christians often attend a worship service just long enough to take the emblems and then exit the church building without hearing the hymns, prayers, praise and sermon that follow. The problem is that the Lord's Supper, although a sublime monument to Jesus' memory, becomes nothing more than an empty form, a meaningless ritual to those who fail to give their heart. Jesus gave us his Supper, not only for a memorial, *but for communion.* Some Christians never give their heart in communion but feel safe merely because they participate at the Lord's table. They live out their lives in a prison of self-delusion.

The problem is that those who seek God in rituals and customs succeed only in laying hold of the outward forms while missing the God concealed in them. Intense focus on the ritual locks out a sense of Presence.

The danger lies not in the outward forms, but in the importance we attach to them. One cannot, after all, live the Christian life without faithful observance of God-given rituals. "Ritual" is not a dirty word. The problem is that we focus so much attention on our forms, customs and traditions, that we fail to see God or even to look in his direction.

Even under Moses' legal system, full of formality and outward forms, God was more interested in the heart than ritual. Joel exhorted the people, "Rend your heart, and not your garments, and turn unto the Lord your God" (Joel 2:13). If the fraud of resting in religious rites was abhorrent under the law, a legal system, how much more abhorrent it is under the gospel, a guileless system that requires more sincerity of spirit.

The message is too plain to misunderstand. Even God-given forms, and there are some, are vain if done without involvement of the heart. Paul complimented the Romans because they had obeyed *from the heart the form* of teaching they had received (Romans 6:17). Our study of the scriptures, debate of orthodox positions, and faithful observance of prayers, sermons, hymns and the Lord's Supper can never generate reverence in a dead heart. Charles Haddon Spurgeon, a noted English preacher of the last century, correctly observed that the outward forms of Christian faith joined with a profane heart are like the garments of Jesus being worn away by his murderers who gambled for them.

Rituals and doctrines, important as they are, can never ignite the soul. Only God can kindle the human spirit. Unless those who faithfully observe religious forms come to know God in personal experience, they will never realize the fire of Presence. They will remain cold, spiritless and anemic.

We must never let our religion satisfy itself with anything less than God. Phillips Brooks gave this good advice:

> Insist on having your soul get at Him and hear His voice. Never, because of the mystery, the awe, perhaps the perplexity and doubt which come with the great experiences, let yourself take refuge in the superficial things of faith.

Purity and Perception

God wants us to see him. We can see him if we will acquire a pure, unpretentious heart. The Old Testament says, "Know the God of your father, and serve Him with a whole heart and a willing mind; for the Lord searches all hearts, and understands every intent of the thoughts. If you seek Him, He will let you find Him" (1 Chronicles 28:9 NASB).

We also read, "For the eyes of the Lord run to and fro throughout the whole earth, to shew himself strong in the behalf of them whose heart is perfect toward him" (2 Chronicles 16:9).

God said through Jeremiah, "I the Lord search the heart, I try the reins, even to give every man according to his ways, and according to the fruit of his doings" (Jeremiah 17:10).

There is a connection between *being and seeing*. Plotinus, a third century philosopher, wrote the following powerful passage:

> They say to us: "Look to God." But it is useless merely to affirm this unless they can tell us how we are to look to Him. And it might be asked, what is to prevent us from looking to God, while at the same time freely satisfying our sensual appetites and not restraining our angry passions. Virtue perfected, enlightened, and deeply rooted in the soul will reveal God to us, but without it He will be an empty name.

When anyone came seeking God, Jesus confronted that person with an ethical demand. When the woman of Samaria inquired about the water of life, Jesus issued a command that struck at the heart of her moral failure: "Go, call thy husband, and come hither" (John 4:16).

When the rich young ruler came asking, "Good Master, what shall I do to inherit eternal life?," Jesus pointed to his problem of covetousness and answered, "Sell that thou hast, and give to the poor" (Matthew 19:21).

When Nicodemus came to Jesus seeking the teacher whose power came from God, Jesus confronted him with, "Verily, verily, I say unto thee, Except a man be born again, he cannot see the kingdom of God" (John 3:3).

David put it like this: "If I regard iniquity in my heart, the Lord will not hear me" (Psalm 66:18).

Who Are the Pure in Heart?

To understand what it means to be pure in heart, we must bear in mind that to be impure does not depend upon the kind or enormity of the sinful deeds we may commit. Adam and Eve, by eating of the forbidden fruit, committed a transgression that seems unimportant when compared with some of the heinous sins reported in the daily newspapers. The first sin was not so serious as murder, immorality, stealing or deliberate falsehood. Yet, the first sin was serious enough to separate Adam and Eve from God.

One may steal an apple. Another may embezzle a million dollars. Both are guilty—not of stealing something great or small—but of stealing. The thing that obscures God is that we are disobedient.

We cannot console a biting conscience with the thought that our sins are not as serious as those of other people. It will not do, for example, if you have a bad temper, to conclude that your weakness is a mere family failure unworthy of consideration. You may say that your grouchy disposition does not warrant the concern of sins like immorality and drunkenness. According to the Scriptures, however, a bad temper is a sin against love which "suffers long." The sin is also against God, for "God is love."

> *Rituals and doctrines, important as they are, can never ignite the soul. Only God can kindle the human spirit.*

The pure in heart know there are no insignificant sins.

Purity and Pretentiousness

The pure in heart are also unpretentious. Spurgeon once said, "When you see a man with a great deal of religion displayed in his shop window, you may depend upon it, he keeps a very small stock of it within."

The more sincerely religious a person is, the less he affects the air of a saint. The most noble believer pretends less because there is less to pretend to. That which is natural never pretends.

An African proverb tells about a frog that tried to look as big as an elephant; it burst. The pure in heart never appear ridiculous. They remain unaffected.

You may have concluded by now that to be pure of heart is virtually impossible. You may be thinking: "Edwin, I want to see God, but I am too weak and impure. I cannot mature enough to enter God's presence." This idea is not true! If your heart's desire is to perceive God, you will realize your goal.

Harry Emerson Fosdick, a noted American preacher and theologian, also gives this good advice:

God does not demand the end when only the beginning is possible, does not scorn the dawn because it is not noon. He welcomes the first movement of man's spirit toward him, not for the fruit which yet is unmatured, but for the seed which still is in the germ.

One must make a beginning, join the clan of seekers. The seeker is blessed equally with the finder. In the process of seeking, one becomes something noble, and in the end, the one who searches always finds.

Questions for Discussion

1. What does it mean to be pure in heart?
2. What is meant by the phrase "being and seeing"?
3. Do you agree that true religion is more inward than outward? Why?
4. Is it always wrong to keep the rituals and traditions of religion? Why?
5. When is it good to observe the outward forms of religion?
6. When do the outward forms of religion become a hindrance?
7. Why is God so concerned about the heart?
8. Is it possible to have a pure heart? How?
9. Is it more important to seek God or find him? Explain.
10. How do the pure in heart see God? When do they see God, later in eternity or now? Could it be both now and later? Explain.

CHAPTER 7

Hiding in the Husks

Phillips Brooks, an American preacher respected for his charm and spiritual qualities, wrote the following paragraphs 106 years ago. In my opinion these ideas are more appropriate for our age than his:

> The great danger facing all of us—let me say it again, for one feels it tremendously—is not that we shall make an absolute failure of life, nor that we shall fall into outright viciousness, nor that we shall be terribly unhappy, nor that we shall feel life has no meaning at all—not these things. The danger is that we may fail to perceive life's greatest meaning, fall short of its highest good, miss the deepest and most abiding happiness, be unable to tender the most needed service, be unconscious of life ablaze with the light of the Presence of God—and be content to have it so—that is the danger.
>
> That some day we may wake up and find that always we have been busy with husks and trappings of life and have really missed life itself. For life without God, to one who has known the richness and joy of life with Him, is unthinkable, impossible. That is what one prays one's friends may be spared—satisfaction with a life that falls short of the best, that has in it no tingle or thrill which comes from a friendship with the Father.

That some day you or I may come to the realization that we have been busy with the "husks and trappings of life" and have missed life itself is a frightening possibility that lies at the root of my motivation for writing this book. Life is too precious to waste in unplanned, hit-or-miss activities.

When we reduce life to its essentials, only one thing is needful—*to have God.* The noblest use of life is to spend it in the pursuit of further knowledge of God. To use our lives in this way—to embark on a journey to find the answer to Job's question, "Oh that I knew where I might find Him"—is to begin an exciting quest that provides a lifetime of spiritual adventure. Those who pursue Presence may or may not have quantity of years, but they always have quality of days.

If we live for this life only, for its frills and fluff, for parting pleasures and fleeting joys, then inevitably we someday will become frustrated with a life that hardly seems worth the price we have to pay to live it. Life spent in pursuit of baubles and bubbles ends in bitter disappointment. Baubles tarnish, and bubbles burst.

In a statement reminiscent of Solomon's conclusions in the book of Ecclesiastes, the Caliph Abdelraham of Spain once said: "I have now reigned above fifty years in victory or peace, beloved by my subjects, dreaded by my enemies, and respected by my allies. Riches and honors, power and pleasure have waited on my call, nor does any earthly blessing appear to have been wanting to my felicity. In this situation, I have diligently numbered the days of pure and genuine happiness which have fallen to my lot; they amount to fourteen. O man, place not thy confidence in this present world!"

Edward Gibbon, best remembered for his history of *The Decline and Fall of the Roman Empire* (6 vols., 1776-88), upon becoming aware of the Caliph's statement, said, "If I may speak of myself, my happy hours have far exceeded, and far exceed, the scanty numbers of the Caliph of Spain; and I shall not scruple to add, that many of them are due to the pleasing labor of composing my history."

Gibbon says, in effect, that life finds meaning not in the acquisition of wealth and power, but in constructive activity. I agree. I must warn you, however, that even worthwhile activity, like that of writing a history, is insignificant when compared with the activity of pursuing God. The greatest and highest road of human welfare and happiness lies along the highway of steadfast pursuit of Presence and not the pursuit of worldly activity or pleasure.

A Charge to the Rich

A life of material ease, creature comfort and worldly activity cannot bring lasting peace of mind. Paul instructed Timothy to "Charge them that are rich in this world, that they be not high-minded, nor trust in uncertain riches, but in the living God, who giveth us richly all things to enjoy" (1 Timothy 6:17).

Paul's warning is plain. Great material wealth tends to make us feel self-sufficient, self-satisfied, spiritually lazy, and indifferent toward God. The real danger of a life of convenience and ease is that it often produces a false security that leads to spiritual death.

Worldly abundance is like a serpent that is harmless if you know how to take hold of it, but if you do not take hold of it properly, it will wrap around your arm and bite you. Wealth in the pocket of an individual who does not love God above all is a very heavy curse. Men pursue riches under the notion that their possessions will set them at ease and above the world. The problem is that those who trust material abundance to adequately serve their every need, finish by becoming slaves themselves. Possessions become the possessors. Those who believe there can be no independence without wealth, in the end, have wealth without independence.

I have read that the seagulls of the Oregon coast originally searched for food far out over the Pacific. When the salmon-canning industry developed on the Columbia River, they began feeding on the great amount of waste from the canning plants. When the plants finally shut down, the gulls had so lost their instinct and will to fly that they starved to death by the hundreds.

In a similar way, a life of ease and creature comfort always has the potential to rob us of our dependence on God and to destroy us spiritually. We can find security only by refusing to hide from God among the husks and trappings of life.

Other Husks and Trappings

Not only do we hide from God in our materialism, we also hide from him in a self-pride that makes it impossible for us to repent. Of all God's commands, repentance is undoubtedly the most difficult to obey. Repentance is the only command that requires us to look honestly at ourselves, see ourselves for the sinful beings we are, confess our shortcomings, and change our direction.

> *When we reduce life to its essentials, only one thing is needful—to have God.*

Some years ago I preached a sermon about repentance in which I make the point that morality alone does not make us one with God. I boldly announced that "all are sinners, and without repentance, no one can see God." At the conclusion of the worship hour, a woman confronted me to express her embarrassment about the sermon. She explained that she had invited several of her professional friends to attend the church services that morning, that they were present, and that they were outstanding citizens in the community. "I feel betrayed because I brought them here only to hear you call them sinners who need to repent," she concluded. "How can I ever face my friends again? I'll never forgive you for what you've done."

Why do we resent the command to repent? Simply because repentance calls upon us to admit we are on the wrong path and that we need to change our course. We resent and resist being brought face to face with our sinful selves.

The possibility of seeing God, however, can never become a reality for the one who is unwilling to discover the direction in which God is moving and to change the course of his life to go along in the same direction with him.

Morality alone cannot substitute for repentance. When the church was born in Jerusalem, "devout men, out of every nation under heaven," had congregated to observe Pentecost (Acts 2:5). Peter touched their hearts with the story of Jesus,

> *Those who trust material abundance to adequately serve their every need, finish by becoming slaves themselves. Possessions become the possessors.*

and they asked, "What shall we do?" (Acts 2:37). Peter answered, "Repent and be baptized every one of you in the name of Jesus Christ for the remission of sins, and ye shall receive the gift of the Holy Ghost" (Acts 2:38).

The people congregated in Jerusalem to observe Pentecost were devout, but they nevertheless needed to repent in order to please God.

Intellectual Sophistication

Another of the husks and trappings of life that obscures God is sophistication. Many hide from God in their intellectual pretensions. Skepticism becomes a foxhole in which souls hide from Presence. Many, when confronted with their need to make a decision about turning life over to God, excuse themselves by saying, "Intellectual doubts stand in the way."

I heard one such individual object, "Maybe God exists, but maybe he doesn't; you can't prove it one way or another." He went on to say that because God cannot be fully known, he cannot be adequately known. "I can't make a decision about becoming a Christian," he said, "because I'm just not sure God exists; I somewhat believe he does, but I don't know."

The skeptic, however, is inconsistent when he objects that God cannot be known fully and therefore cannot be known adequately. Every day the skeptic makes use

51

of things he does not fully understand. Most do not fully understand the mechanical principles of the internal-combustion engine, but they drive their cars anyway. I doubt that many fully understand the laws of electricity, but they use it to do hundreds of daily tasks.

Only when it comes to God is the skeptic willing to say, "I don't know him fully, therefore I can make no use of him." How do we explain such inconsistency? I suspect that the difficulties in the skeptic's path to God are not intellectual doubts, but some impurity, sin, or hardness of soul. The claim of intellectual doubt is but an excuse for a moral problem.

To be honest with God, ourselves and others is difficult. Therefore, some find it easy to excuse their obligation to God by claiming intellectual doubts when the real problem is rebellion.

Service to Men

Sometimes, service to others becomes one of the husks and trappings of life in which men hide from God. Service to mankind is important, but it can never substitute for giving God a place in the heart.

Among my acquaintances is a man who is active in many civic organizations that do much good for the community through their varied activities. He is especially pleased with his participation in one organization that makes medical care available to crippled children. He often reminds me that the church does not provide its members with such opportunities to serve others. Sadly, I have to agree, but I always warn him that he has an obligation to develop an awareness of God and that he cannot forever hide from Divine Presence behind his community service.

Even religious people sometimes hide from God in their good works. People in pews often content themselves with the busy-work of church life, unaware that their feverish activity is but an effort to evade Presence. Although running errands for God is an important function of the Christian life, the order is *Presence first; errands second.*

In an age when the church proudly boasts of its ministries, someone needs to warn that service in the name of God means nothing if the servant does not know God. Many civic-minded organizations serve the community, and they often do a better job than the church. The church is unique only because it consists of people who, motivated by their deep love for

> *Those who pursue Presence may or may not have quantity of years, but they always have quality of days.*

God, serve others in his name. When we face God in judgment, only one question will burn with importance: Do I love God above all?

Come Out of Hiding

David's life was a torrent of spiritual desire. His psalms ring with cries for Presence. He prayed, "Search me, O God, and know my heart: try me, and know my thoughts: And see if there be any wicked way in me, and lead me in the way everlasting" (Psalm 139:23,24)

As long as we refuse to open our hearts and souls to God's view, we must remain without a sense of Presence. If we would see God, we must take seriously some old advice: "Let us search and try our ways, and turn again to the Lord. Let us lift up our hearts with our hands unto God in the heavens" (Lamentations 3:40,41).

Questions for Discussion

1. What is life's greatest essential?
2. What happens to the person who lives for this life only?
3. Why is it impossible for material wealth to bring peace of mind?
4. Is worldly abundance always evil?
5. How does one hide from God by refusing to repent?

6. Why must one repent to know God?
7. How does the skeptic hide from God?
8. How is the skeptic mistaken in his thinking?
9. How do people hide from God in their good works?
10. How does one make himself known to God?

CHAPTER 8

"Show Me Thy Glory"

"Does God have a face?" My daughter Cindy asked this question just before she started first grade. I was uneasy. How do you explain to a child that God is a spirit who sometimes becomes animated, taking on human attributes, but that he is not physical in any conventional sense of our understanding?

Hoping to satisfy her curiosity, I reluctantly assured Cindy that God does have a face. I then quickly changed the topic of discussion, wanting to shift the train of thought to something else. When children begin to ask questions about God, however, one question seems always to lead to another. Cindy's next question was, "Daddy, can I see God's face?"

Children are acutely aware of God. Adults may have difficulty when children want to see God, but it never occurs to the child that asking about the possibility is improper. Wherever we find children, there God is sought. It seems that the most absorbing ambition and aim of children is to get acquainted with the Almighty. A universal impulse to seek God exists among children. They never doubt that there is a God and that God may be known.

Most believers have not yet learned to think of a spiritual God who must be worshipped spiritually. We mistake the shadow for the substance, the form for Presence, the means of grace for grace itself, and the things that reveal God for his actual glory.

Why do children have such an instinct for God? Maybe because they are so fresh from him.

I want intentionally to solicit everyone to develop a childlike passion for God. The desire to see God is not only possible for adults, but, as we shall see, if we are ever to have a life filled with the power of Presence, it is necessary for us to get about the business of seeking God's face.

Moses' Prayer

Moses never lost his childlike desire for God. His words are different, but the request is the same as that of the little girl who asked, "Daddy, can I see God's face?" Moses prayed, "I beseech Thee, shew me Thy glory" (Exodus 33:18).

With great reverence and devotion, Moses cried out from the depths of his being, "I beseech Thee." His whole heart was in his words, as if his life depended on the answer. "Show me Thy glory" is the request of a man who loved God above all. Moses' deep love sought the actual presence of his beloved. His request to see God was as natural as the river rushing to the sea, a flower being fragrant and climbing toward the sun, or a sick, sad child seeking a father's embrace.

If the form of Moses' prayer is faulty, the prayer's faith and fervor are perfect. If the form is faulty, that does not lessen the spirituality of the prayer or the magnificent spirit that prompted it.

Moses knew what few know today. Most believers have not yet learned to think of a spiritual God who must be worshiped spiritually. Very few in this age of privilege and materialism seek for a spiritual vision of God's glory unaided by material forms. We mistake the shadow for the substance, the form for Presence, the means of grace for grace itself, and the things that reveal God for his actual glory.

Moses wanted to see God—the being who is spiritually discerned—apart from all physical things.

God's Pleasure with Moses

God was so pleased with Moses' request that he answered this way:

> "I will cause all my goodness to pass in front of you, and I will proclaim my name, the Lord, in your presence. I will have mercy on whom I will have mercy, and I will have compassion on whom I will have compassion. But," he said, "you cannot see my face, for no one may see me and live." Then the Lord said, "There is a place near me where you may stand on a rock. When my glory passes by, I will put you in a cleft in the rock and cover you with my hand until I have passed by. Then I will remove my hand and you will see my back; but my face must not be seen" (Exodus 33:19-23).

What God reserved from Moses he has reserved from all men. No man has seen the face of God except the Son, but God was so pleased with Moses' spirit that he granted to him the greatest revelation possible for man to receive.

What are we to conclude? It satisfies God when we seek the highest manifestation possible of his glory, and he blesses the sincere search for spiritual sight and understanding. So God said to Moses:

> Be ready in the morning, and then come up on Mount Sinai. Present yourself to me there on top of the mountain . . . . Then the Lord came down in the cloud and stood there with him and proclaimed his name, the LORD. And he passed in front of Moses, proclaiming, "The LORD, the LORD, the compassionate and gracious God, slow to anger, abounding in love and faithfulness, maintaining love to thousands, and forgiving wickedness, rebellion and sin. Yet he does not leave the guilty unpunished; he punishes the children for the sin of the

fathers to the third and fourth generation"
(Exodus 34:2,5-7).

Moses' Attitude

God respected Moses' longing for Presence. I believe
God feels the same about all who diligently seek him.
We should therefore consider what qualified Moses to
have a glimpse of God. Moses' spirit made it possible for
him to see God. Moses had a spirit with these traits:

 • **Sincerity.** Moses was the consummate God-
 seeker. His heart and life were pure; he lived
 only to see God; and he saw God only to live
 like God.

 • **Spirituality.** Moses could discern spiritual
 things because he was a spiritual man. Moses'
 mental nature was highly developed, and his
 mind had been well equipped by training in the
 royal house of Egypt, but his spiritual sensitivity
 that made possible a vision of God.

 • **Service.** Moses' desire to serve his people
more effectively moti-
vated him to seek a
higher knowledge of
God. Moses thought that
if he could see God, he
then could lead Israel as
one who looked with the
eyes of God, thought
with the mind of God,
judged with the conscience of God, and loved
with the heart of God.

In the end, we need nothing but God. We must therefore strip down to essentials and pray everyday, "Show me Thy glory." The one who strives to touch, taste and see God will not go unrewarded.

 • **Humility.** God characterized Moses as the
most humble man alive. Haughtiness and holi-
ness cannot stand together. Because Moses had
a childlike, sensitive spirit, he enjoyed the nearer
presence of God.

The Results

The consequences of Moses' vision were glorious:

> Moses bowed to the ground at once and worshiped. "O Lord, if I have found favor in your eyes," he said, "then let the Lord go with us. Although this is a stiff-necked people, forgive our wickedness and our sin, and take us as your inheritance." . . . Then the Lord said to Moses, "Write down these words, for in accordance with these words I have made a covenant with you and with Israel." Moses was there with the Lord forty days and forty nights without eating bread or drinking water. And he wrote on the tablets the words of the covenant—the Ten Commandments. When Moses came down from Mount Sinai with the two tablets of the Testimony in his hands, he was not aware that his face was radiant because he had spoken with the Lord. When Aaron and all the Israelites saw Moses, his face was radiant, and they were afraid to come near him. But Moses called to them; so Aaron and all the leaders of the community came back to him, and he spoke to them. Afterward all the Israelites came near him, and he gave them all the commands the Lord had given him on Mount Sinai (Exodus 34:8,9,27-32).

Transfiguration is always the result of seeing God. To see God is to become godlike. Moses looked with loving eyes upon the glory of God and was unconsciously transformed to its very image.

The secret of transfiguration is to draw so near the heart of God that our whole mental, moral and spiritual being becomes irradiated with his light. In no other way can we live a successful Christian life.

Seek God's Countenance

Undoubtedly, some people will question the possibility

of seeing God. For many God is unknown and unknowable. If God is unknowable, however, he cannot be God. If he does not reveal to us that which benefits us, but keeps it to himself, then God denies himself and is a contradiction. If selfishness is wrong in man, it cannot be right in God. God never hides truth that would help people in the pursuit of happiness.

Although God is not in a form which the physical eye can see, the inner eye of faith plainly incites a sense of Presence for those with spiritual vision.

Our purpose is to glorify God. When created, we received faculties with which to accomplish the task. If God endowed us with useless spiritual faculties and implanted our souls with impulses and powers for which there is no use or satisfaction, he is unkind, unjust and unlike God.

God gave us powers of spiritual perception because he wants us to know and love him above all. We diligently seek God only because he has put the urge within us. David could therefore say, "My soul followeth hard after thee: thy right hand upholdeth me" (Psalm 63:8).

David's God-given urge to seek Presence was powerful, as may be seen in his words, "As the deer pants for streams of water, so my soul pants for you, O God. My soul thirsts for God, for the living God. When can I go and meet with God?" (Psalm 42:1,2).

Like Moses, David wanted to see God's glory. David was undoubtedly aware of God's warning to Moses about the risk of seeing his face. Intense love, however, takes risks. David said, "When thou saidst, Seek ye my face; my heart said unto thee, Thy face, Lord, will I seek" (Psalm 27:8).

The secret of transfiguration is to draw so near the heart of God that our whole mental, moral and spiritual being becomes irradiated with his light.

In the end, we need nothing but God. We must therefore strip down to essentials and pray every day, "Show me Thy glory." The one who strives to touch, taste and see God will not go unrewarded. "Blessed are they which do

60

hunger and thirst after righteousness: for they shall be filled" (Matthew 5:6).

Questions for Discussion

1. How would you answer the question, "Does God have a face?"
2. Is God physical? How do you know?
3. Does God sometimes become animated? Does he sometimes take form? What form does God take?
4. What was Moses requesting when he asked, "Show me Thy glory?"
5. Is it ever right to want to see God? Under what conditions and for what purpose?
6. Why did God refuse to let Moses see his face?
7. Is God pleased with us when we seek him? Why?
8. Why did Moses want to see God?
9. Do you agree that we have a God-given urge to seek God? Why?
10. What did Jesus mean when he said, "Blessed are they which do hunger and thirst after righteousness: for they shall be filled?" (Matthew 5:6).

CHAPTER 9

Presence in the Storm

Job and his friends had faith in a God who ruled his universe with absolute justice. A necessary connection existed between prosperity and piety. God rewarded those who lived virtuously with health and holdings, and He punished the sinner with suffering.

The belief that God always punishes the wicked and rewards the righteous is a comfortable but mistaken view. Calamities such as floods, fires, earthquakes and disease beset the good and bad alike. The evil and corrupt are often the most fortunate and prosperous members of a society where good men suffer. Divine retribution for sin and reward for righteousness sometimes will have to wait for eternity. Suffering while on earth is no sure sign of sin, and prosperity or good fortune is no sure proof that one is in the clear with God.

Job's friends, however, were convinced that suffering was a sure sign of sin. They therefore accused Job of wickedness. Elihu, reticent because of his youth, listened to the arguments of Job's older friends and finally concluded, "Great men are not always wise . . ." (Job 32:9).

Elihu spoke of those who were great in age as the parallel line in Job 32:9 shows. Owing to his youth, Elihu felt he should keep silent and allow older men with more experience to answer the question of Job. He held back and did not declare his opinion (Job 32:6). Elihu reasoned, "Days should speak, and multitude of years should teach wisdom" (Job 32:7).

Unfortunately, longevity does not guarantee the presence of wisdom. Youth has no monopoly on bad judgment. Elihu finally was compelled to get into the debate because of his dissatisfaction with the older men who -condemned Job although they could not refute his arguments (Job 32:11-14). Elihu discovered that wisdom is not necessarily a matter of years (Job 32:6-10).

A Lesson from Job's Friends

Great men, for whatever reason, are not always wise. Prestige, for example, may come to fortune hunters because of great wealth. Such prestige is not a guarantee of authority in any area of life except making money. An ancient poet wrote this:

> Wealth is friends, home, father, brother,
> title to respect, and fame;
> Yes, wealth is held for wisdom—that it
> should be so is shame.

In a similar way, election to political office does not guarantee that one is an expert in any process except that of winning elections. One is not an expert in morals, methods, or manners, because of one notable accomplishment. Therefore, one shows wisdom in passing pronouncements of the rich, famous and highly educated through analysis, debate, and the observation of time.

Let's again consider Job's friends. They were great men, but they also were mistaken in their view that God always rewards the righteous with prosperity and good health.

Job's Problem

Job shared the conclusions of his friends. He, too, believed that God rewards the righteous and punishes the wicked. For this reason Job questioned God for the way he treated him. Job believed he was upright and perfect. Why should a righteous man suffer such outrageous calamity?

"Does man dare to question God?" is the real question of the book of Job. The book does not, as we have supposed, solve the problem of inexplicable pain and

suffering. Anyone who goes to Job for an answer to the problem of human suffering must always come away with the feeling that he has learned nothing.

Job and Presence

In its effort to teach the futility of questioning God, the book of Job makes a contribution to the idea of Presence. A sense of Presence, not the problem of human suffering, lies at the heart of the book of Job.

Feeling impoverished and bereaved, "opened Job his mouth, and cursed his day" (Job 3:1). Job was so brazen that he accused God of being barbaric and ruthless:

> All was well with me, but he shattered me; he seized me by the neck and crushed me. He has made me his target; his archers surround me. Without pity, he pierces my kidneys and spills my gall on the ground (Job 16:12,13).

Job loudly protested sickness, persecution and ostracism, but a *lack of Presence* aggravated him most of all. Impatiently he asked God, "Why do you hide your face and consider me your enemy" (Job 13:24)?

Suffering while on earth is no sure sign of sin, and prosperity or good fortune is no sure proof that one is in the clear with God.

An appalling misunderstanding, as Job saw it, kept him and God apart. Mortals cannot force the presence of God, but Job nevertheless wished for a mediator to bring him and God together where he might defend his ways to God's face (Job 9:33,34).

Job longed to end his spiritual loneliness. He cried out for Presence:

> If only I knew where to find him; if only I could go to his dwelling! I would state my case before him and fill my mouth with arguments. I would find out what he would answer me, and consider what he would say . . . But if I go to the east, he is not there; if I go to the west, I do not

find him. When he is at work in the north, I do not see him; when he turns to the south, I catch no glimpse of him (Job 23:3-5,8,9).

Job could not understand God giving him the silent treatment, but he believed that someday, perhaps too late, God would come to his senses. "You will search for me," Job said, "but I will be no more" (Job 7:21). Nevertheless, "I know that my Redeemer lives, and that in the end he will stand upon the earth. And after my skin has been destroyed, yet in my flesh I will see God; I myself will see him with my own eyes—I, and not another. How my heart yearns within me!" (Job 19:25-27).

Until the end of the story, Job never weakened in his hope of seeing God. The sad part is that Job wanted to see God on his own terms, but his desire is undeniable:

"Oh, that I had someone to hear me! I sign now my defense—let the Almighty answer me; let my accuser put his indictment in writing. Surely I would wear it on my shoulder, I would put it on like a crown. I would give him an account of my every step; like a prince I would approach him" (Job 31:35-37).

When God finally presented himself to Job, God, not Job, asked questions. Job learned the hard way that one never questions God; God can only be God when God is independent from human conceptions and limitations. God asked,

Would you discredit my justice? Would you condemn me to justify yourself? Do you have an arm like God's, and can your voice thunder like his? Then adorn yourself with glory and splendor, and clothe yourself in honor and majesty. Unleash the fury of your wrath, look at every proud man and bring him low, look at every proud man and humble him, crush the wicked where they stand. Bury them all in the dust together; shroud their faces in the grave.

Then I myself will admit to you that your own right hand can save you (Job 40:8-14).

The Luminous Darkness

Job's mistake was the pride of self-deification. When brought face to face with God, he grieved over a self-pride built upon the foundation of his supposed superior morality.

Job had sought the Presence for egocentric reasons. He wanted to vindicate himself. The fact remains, however, that Job's desire to see God carried him through the dark abyss of outrageous calamity and suffering. Because of his longing for Presence, Job's dark days had a luminous quality which kept him from getting lost.

In a similar way, Paul's sense of Presence kept him from breaking under the load of trial. Paul lived life on the ragged edge. He often escaped destruction by the narrowest margin. At Malta he swam ashore on a piece of wreckage, barely escaping a death by drowning. In humiliation, Paul escaped his enemies at Damascus by sneaking over the city wall in a basket. At Ephesus, he escaped the madness of a whole heathen city only because friends persuaded him not to enter the city's theater where a mob cried out against him for two hours. The disciples took Paul for dead after a stoning at Lystra. Paul's life was one long, difficult fight with persecution, storms at sea, and the powers of evil.

When we find ourselves in the vortex of the storm, only a sense of Presence can calm the tempest.

Paul was aware of his life's conflicts and narrow margins of escape. He once commented that he and his co-workers were "hard pressed on every side, but not crushed; perplexed, but not in despair; persecuted, but not abandoned; struck down, but not destroyed" (2 Corinthians 4:8,9). The apostle went on to say, "We always carry around in our body the death of Jesus, so that the life of Jesus may also be revealed in our body" (2 Corinthians 4:10).

66

Being "hard pressed on every side, but not crushed" pictures someone pressed on every side by an ever-tightening circle of enemies and, yet, able to escape because God makes an opening just wide enough to get through. In other words, enemies crowded and pressed the apostle but never overcame him.

"Perplexed, but not in despair" is a phrase that portrays one whose road is pitch black and unexplored; yet, as he speeds on, God provides just enough light to see the next few feet.

"Persecuted, but not abandoned" depicts the desperation of one being hotly chased by a deadly enemy but not quite overcome because God always comes to his defense at the last possible moment.

"Struck down, but not destroyed" is the drama of one whose enemy has caught up to him and knocked him down but has not knocked him out. The enemy has run down the apostle but has not run him over.

"We always carry around in our body the death of Jesus, so that the life of Jesus may also be revealed in our body" is a phrase that pictures the agony of one who sustains the death wounds of Jesus in his own body. Yet, he never dies himself because "the life of Jesus" comes to his aid. Paul's life was like Moses' burning bush. The apostle always was burning but never engulfed.

Paul also suffered with a physical problem that he called "a thorn in the flesh." Although he prayed fervently for relief, he continued to suffer. God's only answer to the apostle's prayer was, "My grace is sufficient for thee." Paul gladly accepted God's grace, and in a sense of Presence, found strength to weather the storm.

A sense of Presence always helps us cope with life's disasters. Sooner or later, we all must find ourselves in Job's position. The nature of life is for things to go wrong. Like Job, we may lose our families. Perhaps we will encounter financial reverses. Maybe a child will become alarmingly ill. Perhaps a doctor will say the dreaded word "cancer." When we find ourselves in the vortex of the storm, only a sense of Presence can calm the tempest.

Life ceases; wealth slides away; popularity is inconstant; the senses deteriorate; the world changes; and friends die. One alone is dependable. One alone is true to us. One alone can supply our needs. One alone can give a meaning to our complex and intricate nature. One alone can give us calmness and composure. One alone can shape and keep us.

No matter what happens, a sense of Presence will see us through. "For the eyes of the Lord run to and fro throughout the whole earth, to shew himself strong in the behalf of them whose heart is perfect toward him" (2 Chronicles 16:9).

Questions for Discussion

1. Does God always reward the righteous with good health and wealth? Do the wicked always suffer? Why?
2. Are the wealthy and famous always wise? Explain.
3. Are the young always foolish? Do older people always have good judgment? Think of examples from the Bible.
4. Why is it important to carefully examine the conclusions of important people?
5. Do you agree that the idea of Presence, not human suffering, is the theme of Job? Why?
6. What was Job's problem?
7. May we ever question God? May morally good people make demands of God?
8. How does a sense of Presence help us in our suffering?
9. Is it possible to believe that the "eyes of the Lord run to and fro throughout the whole earth, to shew himself strong in the behalf of them whose heart is perfect toward him" (2 Chronicles 16:9)? Why?
10. What does it mean to have a "perfect heart" toward God?

CHAPTER 10

Presence and Purpose

Old Eastern tale recounts the fate of a traveler who happened upon a vicious monster. To save his life the traveler takes refuge in a dry well. As he jumps into the well, he sees a dragon below with his mouth open to devour him. To escape the beast above and the dragon below, he holds onto a twig growing out of a crack in the wall. As he evaluates his position, the traveler notices that two mice are nibbling at the base of the twig. He quickly comes to the sober realization that his life-saving support soon will be eaten away and that he will fall to his doom. He also notices some drops of honey on the leaves of the twig and begins to lick them, knowing that death is inevitable, but wanting to get whatever momentary pleasure may be left.

The enraged beast above and the dragon below are waiting for us all. The mice already are eating away at our lifeline. Sooner or later, we must all die. Death is inescapable. What is the answer to the problem of death?

Secularism

Secularism says the answer to death is to "forget it." The way to forget death is to be busy, useful, committed to noble things and building a better world. Secularism, a religion that finds its purpose in affirming life, denies death. Death is natural, but unpleasant. Therefore, the only answer to death is denial and forgetfulness.

One inescapable fact remains, however: Die we must and die we shall. When one at last comes face to face with death, he cannot possibly put it out of mind.

Epicureanism

The pleasure seekers provide us with another answer to the problem of death: "You only go around once, so grab all the gusto you can."

Should we eat, drink and be merry today, knowing that tomorrow we die? Should we lick the honey from the leaves until the last possible moment? Should we, because of impending death, admit the hopelessness of life and squeeze it for all the pleasure that may be in reach?

Death does not rob life of purpose; death is life's purpose.

Far from easing life's frustrations with death and other problems, worldly pleasure only multiplies our pain. The Epicurean answer to the problem of death may satisfy the thoughtless pleasure seeker, but the rational, even among unbelievers, believe that only the intellectually dull could pursue the last drop of honey while death knocks at the door.

Death and Purpose

If, however, those without a sense of Presence, no matter how discerning, reject the hedonist's answer to death, then nothing is left. Precisely for this reason many thinkers have concluded that life is a deception.

The English philosopher and mathematician Bertrand Russell, for example, thought that human existence is not worthwhile because death ultimately robs life of its achievements. Not only does the individual die, but the entire human race eventually must cease to exist. Life is, therefore, a hoax.

Schopenhauer, another philosopher without a sense of Presence, concluded that it is ridiculous to think of life as a gift. He thought that we would all have turned down such a gift if we had been able to examine it beforehand. Given our choice, we would want to be left in the tranquillity of oblivion. Death, the final "judgment of nature" is proof that life is a "false path."

Without a sense of Presence, life always must seem without meaning. If all our dreams and accomplishments vanish in death and dissolve into extinction, nothing is worth our effort. Without God life is, as Tolstoy put it, a "stupid fraud." Nothing is worth undertaking.

For the one, however, who spends life in the pursuit of Presence, death, far from robbing life of purpose, is only the final step of a lifelong journey into the very throne room of God. Death is a welcome guest because the goal or purpose toward which all life was directed is finally

In deep trials or great joy, a sense of Presence always gives purpose to life.

achieved. The psalmist put it this way: "As for me, I will behold thy face in righteousness: I shall be satisfied, when I awake, with thy likeness" (Psalm 17:15).

For the God stalker, life without death would be the "false path." Death does not rob life of purpose; death is life's purpose.

The Forgotten God

The desire for Presence infuses both life and death with purpose. That leads me to my problem. I cannot help noticing that many believers neither live, nor die, well. Therefore, I have no alternative but to conclude that this generation of Christians as a whole has no sense of Presence. A good case can be made for the idea that many have forgotten God entirely.

In his 1983 acceptance speech of the Templeton Prize in Religion, Alexander Solzhenitsyn forcefully stated a conviction that the calamitous revolution that swallowed 60 million Russian people was the result of men forgetting God. Solzhenitsyn went further to say that the essential feature of the entire 20th century is that men have forgotten God.

If forgetting God has resulted in atheism and communism for Russia, a rapacious appetite for material things is the result in the West. Take me seriously. Our society, including most of the church, has forgotten God. Some believers will object that to forget something so fundamental as God is impossible. Some will argue that you cannot forget God like you forget the grocery list or your wallet. The fact remains that most of us have placed God somewhere and forgotten where we put him.

If God has not been forgotten, how are we to explain the apathy of this church age? Why the lack of purpose? Few seem interested or involved. The attitude toward life is one of despair, absurdity and uselessness. Many feel a dismal sameness about their existence. They keep on keeping on, going to worship and working at the job, but in their spirits is a depression. Many know something is missing in their lives but are at a loss to know what troubles them.

Preachers often go into their pulpits on the Lord's Day feeling rushed and worried about whether their sermons are prepared adequately. They work diligently, but without God-centered effort. They are tense and anxious as they begin preaching, knowing they are not in a state of recollection. No depth of silence and continuity of prayer—no meditative brooding over the scriptures—has preceded their talk. They continue, week after week, disintegrated, distraught and disconnected.

What is the trouble? God is forgotten! There is no sense of Presence.

An Old Problem

Emptiness and despair are not new. Solomon despaired of life 3,000 years ago. He, like many believers in our own materialistic age, sought for meaning of life in riches, and he failed. He tried pleasure, hard work and building. All ended in disappointment. Does this sound familiar?

After searching the world over for something that would give purpose and meaning to life, Solomon concluded, "Vanity of vanities; all is vanity" (Ecclesiastes 1:2). Disillusioned by the hollowness of this materialistic world, he turned in the only possible direction. His final words of relief were, "Let us hear the conclusion of the whole matter: Fear God, and keep his commandments:

for this is the whole duty of man" (Ecclesiastes 12:13). Solomon found purpose only in a *sense of presence.*

God says, "Let not the wise man glory in his wisdom, neither let the mighty man glory in his might, let not the rich man glory in his riches: But let him that glorieth glory in this, that he understandeth and knoweth me, that I am the LORD which exercise loving-kindness, judgment, and righteousness, in the earth: for in these things I delight, saith the Lord" (Jeremiah 9:23,24). Isaiah said,

> Do you not know? Have you not heard? The Lord is the everlasting God, the Creator of the ends of the earth. He will not grow tired or weary, and his understanding no one can fathom. He gives strength to the weary and increases the power of the weak. Even youths grow tired and weary, and young men stumble and fall; but those who hope in the Lord will renew their strength. They will soar on wings like eagles; they will run and not grow weary, they will walk and not be faint (40:28-31).

What Is Life's Purpose?

God must not be simply a part of life; he must be the whole of life.

If you accuse me of being an escapist from reality or of subscribing to a childish philosophy, I can only answer that for 20 years I have been the pulpit minister of a local church, where life is real and often difficult. I remind you also that man in all his wisdom and brilliance has never offered a workable alternative to Solomon's conclusion. We must awaken to the realization that meaning and purpose in life do not lie in materialistic pursuits, but in the pursuit of a sense of Presence.

A sense of Presence does not mean that we withdraw from the world of time, space and human activity. It does mean that we have a permanent, continuous awareness of God, an awareness that has a powerful impact upon human personality and instills an inner security and purpose that are unshakable.

Dietrich Bonhoeffer, a German theologian martyred by Hitler's henchmen, found security and purpose in a sense of Presence when all else

God must not be simply a part of life; he must be the whole of life.

failed. Danger only drove Bonhoeffer to a greater awareness of God. In one of his prison letters, he wrote about his faith concerning a God with whom all things are possible. He stated his belief that no earthly power can hurt us without God's will. He concluded, "One thing is certain: we must always live close to the presence of God . . . ." In whatever ways you may fault Bonhoeffer's theology, you have to admire his sense of Presence.

What worked for Bonhoeffer will work for us all. In deep trials or great joy, a sense of Presence always gives purpose to life.

Questions for Discussion

1. Why is it not possible to solve the problem of death by merely forgetting it?
2. What's wrong with getting all the "gusto" life has to offer?
3. How does the pursuit of worldly pleasure multiply life's difficulties?
4. Does death make life a "hoax"? What is the purpose of death?
5. How is it possible to have an optimistic view of death?
6. How do you account for the apathy of today's church?
7. Has God been forgotten? How do you know?
8. What is the answer to despair?
9. What made Solomon conclude, "Fear God, and keep his commandments: for this is the whole duty of man"?
10. Why is it good advice to fear and obey God?

CHAPTER 11

Jesus and Presence

Laurence Sterne a British author best remembered for his novel, *The Life and Opinions of Tristram Shandy* (9 volumes, 1759-67), fought a brave but losing battle with tuberculosis. Sterne understood the power of well-timed words of consolation. He said, "Before an affliction is digested, consolation comes too soon; after it is digested it comes too late; but there is a mark between these two, as fine almost as a hair, for the comforter to take aim at."

The one who wants to minister to the afflicted must come to grips with the importance of proper timing. My office in downtown Phoenix is located near most of the mortuaries. Because I am available, hundreds of families, religious and non-religious, have asked me to officiate at the memorial services of their loved ones.

My experience with so many bereaved families has taught me that they need comfort most not during the week of the funeral, but later. If, however, I wait too long before visiting those I wish to console, I miss the opportunity forever. The best time to help the bereaved is after they have begun to ponder the meaning of their loss, but before their suffering is fully accepted. In my experience, anywhere from one to six months after the loss of a loved one is the most opportune time to help a sorrowing family see a loving, caring Presence who wishes to share their burdens.

Jesus' Sense of Timing

No one comforts the troubled of heart with the precise

and wonderful sense of timing that Jesus did. Take, for example, the Lord's words of consolation in John 14. At the close of John 13, we find the disciples troubled because of Christ's announcement that he soon would die and ascend back to his Father. The deep sense of absence that the disciples anticipated drove them to despair. Jesus' men felt their world was about to end in chaos.

The entire discourse of John 14 is an effort on Jesus' part to console his disciples in their moment of desperation. Jesus' timing was perfect. He aimed for and hit Sterne's "mark . . . as fine almost as a hair." The disciples were just beginning to digest the idea that Jesus must die, but the full impact of Christ's absence would not be felt for a few more days. The disciples had begun to digest their affliction, but it had not yet been fully digested.

At just the right time for maximum effect, Jesus gave a soothing discourse meant to reinforce his exhortation. He said, "Let not your heart be troubled," a statement he made twice (John 14:1,27).

Nowhere is recorded a more appropriate, wonderful, sensitive, and so adapted to produce comfort and consolation as John 14. Jesus not only told his disciples to have untroubled hearts, but he also made several promises that would ensure peace.

Reunion

First, Jesus assured the disciples that his departure was not to be a permanent separation (vv. 1-3). The Lord was going away to prepare a place for the disciples in his Father's house. Upon completion of the place, Jesus would return to receive his followers.

I find it interesting that Jesus did not say, "And when I go to prepare a place for you, I will come again and take you to that place." Instead, Jesus said something more comforting: "I will come again, and receive you unto myself . . . ." Jesus promised to take the disciples, not to a place, *but into his embrace.* What comfort!

The disciples were about to lose their Master. These

76

men had been in the presence of Christ constantly since the beginning of his public ministry. The sense of absence was already unbearable.

Having told his men that their destiny involved a place and his embrace, Jesus announced to the disciples that they knew the way to the place he was going (v. 4).

The Way

Thomas, speaking for the group, replied, "Lord, we know not whither thou goest; and how can we know the way?" (v. 5). Jesus then said, "I am the way, the truth, and the life: no man cometh unto the Father, but by me" (v. 6).

Have you ever been lost? I was hopelessly lost once in Amsterdam. I asked directions, but because I could not speak the language well, no one understood my problem. When a friendly face said in words I understood, "I'm going your way, and I'll take you where you want to go," he became the way for me.

A deep sense of Presence enables one to say, "I will do God's will as I see it, and God will use it to his glory."

If Jesus is "the way" for his followers, then he must be present. For someone absent to be the way to any destination is impossible.

Prayer

Furthermore, the Lord said, "And I will do whatever you ask in my name, so that the Son may bring glory to the Father" (v. 13). Jesus' promise, "I will do whatever you ask," implies Presence. The Lord will be absent physically, but Presence will hear and answer the disciples' prayers.

Prayer is often made cheap and brought to low levels by the selfish who make demands of God, but it remains the most effective way to achieve a sense of Presence. At the turn of this century, Thomas Talmage, a Presbyterian clergyman known for his dramatic preaching, made this wonderful observation in a sermon:

> When a soul prays, God does not sit upright until the prayer travels immensity and climbs to his ear. In more than one place the Psalmist said He inclined His ear, by which I come to believe that God puts His ear so closely down to your lips that he can hear your faintest whisper. It is not God away off up yonder; it is God away down here, close up—so close up that when you pray to him it is not more a whisper than a kiss.

Prayer is not just the informing of God about our needs. He already knows our needs. To pray is to open oneself to the promptings of God. In the language of Thomas Carlyle, "Prayer is the aspiration of our poor, struggling, heavy-laden soul toward its Eternal Father."

I do not, however, want to leave the impression that it is wrong to take our needs to God in prayer. Some may ask, "If God already knows what we want and need, why tell him?" The answer is because our relationship with the Father is personal. As a parent, I want my children to open their hearts to me without fear, though much of what they may say already is known.

Prayer is relationship—a language in which the human spirit asks God to take it lovingly to his own heart. In prayer, one turns his mind and heart to God. To pray is to stand in the awareness of Presence, conversing about our needs, hopes, dreams, fears, or anything else a child may wish to discuss with his Father.

Devastated by the prospect of Christ's departure from the world, Jesus could offer the disciples no greater comfort than to say he would answer their prayers. In order for Jesus to keep his promise to grant all their prayer requests, he would have to be near the disciples, aware of their needs, and listening when they felt the urge to draw near to Presence.

Another Presence

There's more. Jesus promised a new Presence: "I will

pray the Father, and he shall give you another Comforter, that he may abide with you for ever" (v. 16).

The Greek word for "Comforter" is *parakletos. Parakletos* is a difficult word to translate because no single English word conveys the Greek meaning. *Parakletos* is a legal word that signifies a friend of the accused who served as advocate and counsel for the defense and testifies to his friend's character when others wish to condemn him. *Parakletos* occurs once in this way when John writes about Jesus (1 John 2:1). John was calling Jesus our "advocate" with the Father.

Parakletos means "one who is called in." The "one who is called in" is to do something or render some service. The implication is that the Holy Spirit is the helper of men.

Parakletos is a word often used to speak about the type of help that keeps men on their feet when they would fall if left to themselves.

Jesus' promise to send another Presence enriched the disciples. When the promised "Comforter" (Helper, Advocate) came, the Twelve had, not one, but two Helpers. With two Helpers, the disciples could go past the breaking point without breaking.

Peace

Finally, Jesus told his disciples that, in his physical absence, they will have peace of heart (v. 27). In this connection is a superficial but interesting resemblance between Epicureanism and what Christ offers his followers. Epicurus, a Greek philosopher (341-270 B.C.), defined philosophy as the art of making life happy, strictly subordinating metaphysics to ethics, with pleasure as the highest and only good. For Epicurus, pleasure was not heedless indulgence, but *ataraxia* (serenity), manifesting itself in the avoidance of pain.

Epicureanism places a high premium on being calm and unperturbed in all life's varied circumstances. A difference is obvious, however, between what Christ offers and what Epicureanism offers. Epicureanism says that undisturbed life is possible because "the gods, if they exist at all, take no notice of us." Christ, on the other hand, says we have peace because God does take notice of us, loves us, and hears our prayers. The apostle Paul makes the point powerfully:

> Do not be anxious about anything, but in everything, by prayer and petition, with thanksgiving, present your requests to God. And the peace of God, which transcends all understanding, will guard your hearts and your minds in Christ Jesus (Philippians 4:6,7).

Peace always follows Presence. Presence means peace for the reasons listed below.

In Presence, we lose our fear of getting lost. Have you ever wondered how a pilot is able to fly his airplane over unfamiliar territory without getting lost? He can do so because of mapped, numbered highways in the sky. If an airplane's instruments are properly set, the pilot has no fear of getting lost, for his airplane is mechanically in the right path, and he knows his course is correct, though he may not recognize a single landmark.

To pray is to stand in the awareness of Presence, conversing about our needs, hopes, dreams, fears, or anything else a child may wish to discuss with his Father.

In a similar way, birds fly incredible distances over the ocean with no fear of losing their way. The Arctic tern, for example, leaves the Arctic in August to spend our winter months in Antarctica, and returns to the Arctic in June—a round trip of 22,000 miles over uncharted oceans. Are such fragile creatures courageous? Probably not. They have no fear of getting lost because they are mechanically in the will of God; they will not lose the way.

Because of Presence, no true believer loses his way.

Presence removes the burden of responsibility for what happens in our lives of service. When the believer does God's will, God carries the burden of consequences. Presence means we do not have to worry about the seeming little fruit our lives produce. We plant and water, and Presence takes care of the increase.

Presence resolves our conflicts. Shall I do this, that or something else? One can make such decisions easily if the questions are about matters that are plainly right or wrong. Often, however, we have to decide one course of action when many equally good options are available. What then? We can lose a lot of sleep worrying about what to do with our opportunities.

Presence resolves the problem. A deep sense of Presence enables one to say, "I will do God's will as I see it, and God will use it to his glory."

We Are Not Alone

Jesus' consoling words in John 14 show a love of the most tender and self-forgetful nature. When Christ spoke these words, he was troubled deeply himself. We read in John 13, "When Jesus had thus said, he was troubled in spirit, and testified, and said, Verily, verily, I say unto you, that one of you shall betray me" (v. 21).

Why would the agonizing Shepherd, facing the cross, take time to comfort his flock? Part of the answer to our question may be that Jesus was, by nature, gentle and kind. I believe, however, that Jesus also wanted to impress his followers, including us, with the knowledge that *no believer is ever left alone.*

The only thing that remains is for us to follow the example of the psalmist who said, "I have set the Lord always before me: because he is at my right hand, I shall not be moved" (Psalm 16:8).

Questions for Discussion

1. Why is John 14 an exhortation of consolation?
2. How is Jesus the way to God?
3. What did Jesus mean when he said, "I will do whatever you ask in my name that the Son may bring glory to the Father"?

4. Why is prayer a good way to achieve a sense of Presence?
5. If God already knows our needs, why pray?
6. Why is prayer a relationship?
7. Why did Jesus send the Holy Spirit?
8. In what way is Epicureanism like Christianity?
9. In what way is Epicureanism unlike Christianity?
10. Why does a sense of Presence instill peace?

CHAPTER 12

Jehovah Is There

Among the Hebrew names for God is the name *Jehovah-shammah*, which means "Jehovah is there" (Ezekiel 48:35). Ezekiel prophesied during some of the darkest days of Israel's history. The temple was in ruins; national pride was broken; and only a pitiful remnant remained in the Jewish homeland.

Ezekiel, who delivered all his prophecies when in captivity, had predicted the destruction of the temple. Now he brings a prophecy of hope and anticipation. He predicts the restoration of the people, their religious and political institutions, and their land in a measure to equal the past. The guarantee of Ezekiel's utterance of prophetic hope is the name *Jehovah-shammah*—"Jehovah is there." He promises them a sense of Presence.

In keeping with his promise, Jehovah *was* there when Zechariah initiated his series of messages to encourage the people of Judah in their efforts to rebuild the temple. Many enemies were around, and the difficulties seemed insurmountable, but Judah succeeded because Jehovah was there. What Judah accomplished was "Not by might, nor by power, but by my spirit, saith the LORD of hosts" (Zechariah 4:6).

At many points in Israel's history, Jehovah was there. Jehovah was there when Israel entered Canaan. Without Presence, Israel would never have possessed the Promised Land. The obstacles were too many and too great for Israel to succeed alone. As one example, consider the crossing of the Jordan River. The Jordan was at flood level. How would 2 million people transport themselves across a river whose water was, by the estimate of some, 100 feet deep? Jehovah was there to provide an answer. He instructed the priests to enter the river carrying the ark, and upon their entry into the Jordan, the waters divided. While the priests stood in the river bed, all the people crossed over on hard ground.

I find it interesting that God promised to divide the waters of the Jordan precisely when "the soles of the feet of the priests . . . shall rest in the waters" (Joshua 3:13). If the priests had come to the water's edge and then stopped for the water to divide, they would be standing there yet. Only after stepping into the water was the water cut off and rolled back.

John Greenleaf Whittier, an American Quaker poet and reformer, correctly observed that "the steps of faith fall on the seeming void, but find the rock beneath." Because Jehovah is there, faith always lights us through the darkness and builds a bridge across the gulf of obstacles that sight and reason can never cross.

Israel crossed the Jordan only because of a great faith in Presence. Jehovah was there.

Moab and Ammon

On another occasion, a vast army of Moabites and Ammonites marched against Judah. Outnumbered, Judah was hopeless to defend itself. Alarmed, King Jehoshaphat proclaimed a fast for all the people. As Jehoshaphat stood in prayer at the temple of the Lord with all the men of Judah, their wives and their children, the Spirit of the Lord came upon Jahaziel, son of Zechariah, and he said, "Hearken ye, all Judah, and ye inhabitants of Jerusalem, and thou king Jehoshaphat, Thus saith the LORD unto you, Be not afraid nor dismayed by reason of this great multitude; for the battle is not yours, but God's" (2 Chronicles 20:15).

Although God instructed the Judahites to prepare for war, he promised them they would not have to fight the battle (2 Chronicles 20:17). Because of God's intervention, the invading armies destroyed each other (2 Chronicles 20:22,23). Fear came upon all the nations when they heard the Lord had fought for Judah. "And the kingdom of Jehoshaphat was at peace, for his God had given him rest on every side" (2 Chronicles 20:30).

Israel's Distinction

Israel was distinguished from all other nations by the presence of a holy God dwelling in its midst. God said to Moses, "My presence shall go with thee, and I will give thee rest." Moses answered, "If thy presence go not with me, carry us not up hence. For wherein shall it be known here that I and thy people have found grace in thy sight? is it not in that thou goest with us? so shall we be separated, I and thy people, from all the people that are upon the face of the earth." God answered Moses, "I will do this thing also that thou hast spoken: for you have found grace in my sight, and I know thee by name" (Exodus 33:14-17).

> *Because Jehovah is there, faith always lights us through the darkness and builds a bridge across the gulf of obstacles that sight and reason can never cross.*

Did you notice Moses' argument that the only way others would know that he and his people had "found grace" in God's sight was for his "presence" to go with them? Did you also notice that God promised his presence because Moses had "found grace" in his sight?

A great truth emerges from the discussion between God and Moses in Exodus 33: *God's grace is a manifestation of his presence and power.*

The apostle Paul had a physical problem that he called a "thorn in the flesh." Paul made his "thorn" the subject of earnest prayer on three different occasions. God's reply was, "My grace is sufficient for thee . . ." (2 Corinthians 12:9). In other words, God told Paul that his presence would empower him to live with his physical problem. The apostle concluded, "Most gladly therefore will I rather glory in my infirmities, that the power of Christ may rest upon me."

The phrase, "My grace is sufficient," implies that the goodwill of God supports the believer with an unseen, but powerful hand. "My grace is sufficient" is a promise. Because *Jehovah is there,* God's power enables us to triumph over all our mental, physical, emotional and spiritual difficulties. God is aware of our lives and circumstances totally and, therefore, is able to help us in our infirmities.

As Paul saw it, the reality of Presence made possible the reality of grace. Grace was therefore power. For the apostle, grace was a divine influence or energy that operated within his Christian nature, empowering him to do his special work. Paul, for example, attributed his apostleship to grace. He said that "it pleased God, who separated me from my mother's womb, and called me by his grace, To reveal his Son in me, that I might preach him among the heathen . . ." (Galatians 1:15,16).

Paul made many other references to God's grace as some special quality that enabled him to fulfill the duties of his apostleship or live a victorious life. Here are a few:

> For I say, through the grace given unto me, to every man that is among you, not to think of himself more highly than he ought to think; but to think soberly, according as God hath dealt to every man the measure of faith (Romans 12:3).

> Nevertheless, brethren, I have written the more boldly unto you in some sort, as putting you in mind, because of the grace that is given to me of God, That I should be the minister of Jesus Christ to the Gentiles, ministering the gospel of God, that the offering up of the Gentiles might be acceptable, being sanctified by the Holy Ghost (Romans 15:15,16).

> According to the grace of God which is given unto me, as a wise masterbuilder, I have laid the foundation, and another buildeth thereon. But let every man take heed how he buildeth thereupon (1 Corinthians 3:10).

But by the grace of God I am what I am: and his grace which was bestowed upon me was not in vain; but I laboured more abundantly than they all: yet not I, but the grace of God which was with me (1 Corinthians 15:10).

Saved by Grace

The power of grace was displayed most significantly in the apostle's life when it reached out to rescue him from sin. When Paul had his conversion experience on the Damascus road, he was a persecutor of the followers of Christ. While on his way to arrest Christians, Christ suddenly seized Paul, irradiated him with Divine light, and rescued him by the grace of a powerful Presence.

Even when the apostle says that grace saves through faith (Ephesians 2:8), he speaks of the faith of a present Christ. Ephesians 2:8,9 alludes to Habbakuk 2:4. The problem is that Paul's quote corresponds neither to the Hebrew text or the Greek text of Habbakuk's passage. The Hebrew Old Testament speaks of one who is "righteous by his [own] faith," and the Greek Old Testament speaks of one who is "righteous by my [God's] faith." Paul omits the pronouns in his New Testament quote.

One possible answer to the problem is to say that Paul intended to convey the meaning that one finds justification because of his own faith, a widely accepted view. A better answer is that Paul intended to say that one obtains justification because of God's faithfulness in the person of Christ. The following Pauline passages, properly translated in the King James Version, powerfully make the point:

> The scriptures hath concluded all under sin, that the promise by faith of Jesus Christ might be given to them that believe (Galatians 3:22).
> In whom we have boldness and access with confidence by the faith of him (Ephesians 3:12).
> And be found in him, not having mine own righteousness, which is of the law, but that which is through the faith of Christ, the righ-

teousness which is of God by faith (Philippians 3:9).

Knowing that a man is not justified by works of the law, but by faith of Jesus Christ, even we have believed in Jesus Christ, that we might be justified by the faith of Christ, and not by works of the law . . . (Galatians 2:16).

I am crucified with Christ: nevertheless I live; yet not I, but Christ liveth in me: and the life which I now live in the flesh I live by the faith of the Son of God, who loved me, and gave himself for me (Galatians 2:20).

Translations that change the above passages to read "faith in Jesus Christ," miss the meaning of the Greek, *Pisteos Iesou Christou,* which literally translates, "faith of Jesus Christ."

The Means of Justification

The ground for justification is never the sinner's faith, but the "faith of the Son of God." The sinner is, of course, to believe in Jesus. Faith in Christ positions the sinner to appropriate the blessings of Christ. Christ's faith, however, is the sinner's only means of salvation.

> *God's grace is so vast that it not only saves everyone who comes to him past, present, future, and for all eternity, but it also provides a means for the Christian to live victoriously.*

Perhaps you noticed that two of the above passages, Galatians 2:16 and Galatians 3:22, spoke of man's faith and the "faith of Christ" in the same context. Either these passages contain a superfluous repetition by combining the Messiah's faith with the sinner's faith, which I think unlikely, or they correlate Christ's faith and the believer's faith, making the point that although the sinner must believe in Jesus, the faith of Christ is that which justifies. This explains how the formula "from faith to faith" (Romans 1:17) represents more than empty rhetoric.

No sincere believer will boast that his faith is a meritorious contribution by which he deserves grace. Deserved grace is a contradiction. God's grace may be appropriated only through the "faith of Jesus Christ." The believer finds justification only in total identification with Jesus. When God looks at Jesus, he sees the believer, for the believer is one with Christ. They are inseparable. Christ is the head. Christians are the body. Believers are saved and safe because of a perfect Presence. The righteousness of Jesus is the very righteousness of the Christian.

Every child of God owes his salvation to God's grace which saves through the "faith of" Presence—the faith of a perfect savior who lived among us, who faithfully faced the ordeal of the cross, who faithfully remains as our helper and intercessor, and who abides within to strengthen us for the hour of trial and temptation.

If you want a deeper sense of Presence, consider the immensity of God's grace. If you want to contemplate God's magnificence, think about the abundance of power with which he fills every believer's life.

God's grace is so vast that it not only saves everyone who comes to him past, present, future, and for all eternity, but it also provides a means for the Christian to live victoriously. Sin seeks to destroy even the believer, "But where sin abounded, grace did much more abound" (Romans 5:20). God's grace exists in abundance. Grace is equal to every challenge of life because it flows from an inexhaustible and powerful source—God's loving presence.

Because *Jehovah is there,* the Christian has peace, confidence and eternal life.

Questions for Discussion

1. What are some of the ways Jehovah was in your life when you needed him?
2. Why is God's grace a sign of his presence?
3. Explain how God's grace is a manifestation of his power?

4. How does grace save us from sin?
5. What role does our faith play in our salvation?
6. What role does the faith of Christ play in our salvation?
7. What does Ephesians 2:8,9 mean to you?
8. What is meant by the phrase, "from faith to faith" in Romans 1:17?
9. How can the righteousness of Christ be the same righteousness of the Christian?
10. What is meant by the phrase in Romans 5:20, "Where sin abounded, grace did much more abound"?

CHAPTER 13

A Formula for Presence

As I begin this final chapter, I want you to know that the ideas it presents were born of my personal struggle to live a faithful Christian life. I became a Christian while yet a teen-ager. Soon after baptism, I developed an interest in preaching and decided, as we often put it, to "give my life to the ministry." The churches immediately provided opportunities for me to preach, and with the enthusiasm and flamboyance characteristic of youth, I managed to be entertaining, if not informative. In time, however, I developed the skills of my trade and became good at my craft.

Then came that Lord's Day morning when I realized that I was in love with preaching, but not with God. Twenty-five years had passed since my baptism. Now, at the age of 40, standing in the pulpit preparing to announce my sermon text, I suddenly was struck with an awareness that God was not real to me. I could not explain why, after so much time, I felt so spiritually empty. I only knew that I no longer could speak for a God I did not know.

Looking back on that day, I recall the temptation either to dismiss the church or to ask the song leader to fill the sermon time with congregational singing. Instead, I continued my old ways and preached a sermon because a sermon needed preaching. That sermon, like all the ones I had preached before it, was a sorry sermon.

An old German proverb says, "There are many preachers who do not listen to themselves." I listened to me for the first time that Sunday morning, and what I heard

91

was embarrassing. I had no sense of Presence. My life and my preaching were inappropriate, hypocritical and sinful. Since then I have developed a sense of Presence, and what I have learned from my experience is when sermons come from the overflow of a heart deeply in love with God, they remain fresh and good years after they are first delivered; however, sermons preached simply because sermons must be preached are stale the next day.

The experience of seeing the emptiness of my soul was the beginning of my quest for God. I resolved to never again speak for a God I did not know and love. What I didn't know at the time was that the process of becoming more aware of God has no end. God searching is a lifelong activity. Whenever I think I am about to get my mind around God, he gets much larger, and the quest has to begin anew. I have come to the realization that to know all there is to know about God is impossible. Yet, one can become totally aware of the Presence, and that awareness of a loving God's nearness makes life a joyful adventure.

Meditation

How do you develop a sense of Presence? From the beginning, those with whom I have discussed this book have encouraged me not to neglect giving a formula, which, if followed, would ensure the reader a greater awareness of God. I am not sure, however, that such a formula for Presence exists. Awareness of God, after all, is a decision of the heart. If you want a greater sense of Presence, you will have to decide to give God first place in your conscious awareness.

I am reluctant to use the word "meditation" because many think of meditation as nothing more than quiet time when the mind becomes thoughtless and the spirit numb. Meditation is useful only when it is dynamic or active.

If a formula for Presence can be given, the first ingredient is making time to think about God—giving him a place in conscious awareness. Does this sound easy? It isn't. One of the rarest of all Christian accomplishments is the ability to engage in profitable meditation. We can go 20 miles to hear a sermon more easily than we can spend five minutes thinking about it when we get home. Such thoughtlessness has resulted in a lack of Christian growth. It isn't hasty listening or rapid reading, but serious meditation upon the truths we hear and read, which make them sweet and profitable to our souls.

> *When you read the Scriptures, never approach them with the thought, "God has spoken." Read with the thought, "God is speaking." God's Word is living and powerful.*

One of our problems is that the society in which we live conditions us not to think or concentrate. We live in a world of bright lights and flashing images. Television, which occupies most of our waking hours, assaults us daily with hundreds of 60-second commercials. Prime-time soap operas, which are television's most popular programs, entertain us with the sordid involvements of several people, never bringing anyone's story to a conclusion and never giving more than a few minutes to anyone's story before shifting to someone else's.

In an age of television, the quick fix, and get-rich-quick thinking, people are too frenzied, jittery and restless to take the time to think. God seekers, however, must take time to reflect on spiritual things. Merely reading the Scriptures, hearing a variety of sermons, and engaging in a great amount of religious conversation are not enough. We must meditate on these things until the truth in them becomes our own. What we read and hear may furnish us with many ideas, but only our thinking about those ideas can form our judgments.

Meditation is the life of the soul because it is that exercise by which the mind recalls known truths as some of God's creatures do their food—to chew upon again until they digest all the valuable parts. Meditation makes it possible for us to turn known truth into owned conviction, to find rest on Jesus' breast, and to commune with God.

The one who meditates most on divine truth always will be the wisest, strongest Christian, and the one who gives God the largest place in his conscious awareness always will have the greatest sense of Presence.

Jesus

Another ingredient in the formula for Presence is Jesus Christ. No sincere Christian desires a greater manifestation of God than Jesus. In Revelation 1:13-16, John describes Jesus by quoting words that refer to the Ancient of Days in Ezekiel 43:2 and Daniel 10:5-7. John sees:

> In the midst of the seven candlesticks one like unto the Son of man, clothed with a garment down to the foot, and girt about the paps with a golden girdle. His head and his hairs were white like wool, as white as snow; and his eyes were as a flame of fire; And his feet like unto fine brass, as if they burned in a furnace; and his voice as the sound of many waters. And he had in his right hand seven stars: and out of his mouth went a sharp two-edged sword: and his countenance was as the sun shineth in his strength.

John says, in effect, that Jesus is God. Every other writer of the New Testament agrees. Paul, for example, says Jesus was in the form of God (Philippians 2:6). In Colossians 2:9, Paul boldly announces that the fullness of God dwells bodily in Jesus. Writing to Titus, the apostle called Jesus our "great God" (Titus 2:13). To Timothy, Paul said that God manifested himself in Jesus' flesh (1 Timothy 3:16).

If you want to know God, become acquainted with Jesus. Read the Gospels of Matthew, Mark, Luke and John once a month. Memorize the biographical sketches of Jesus' life, or at least become very familiar with them.

Learn all you can about Jesus. Love him. Live for him. As Jesus comes into sharper focus, so will God.

Some of the most emotionally moving truths I know about God, I learned in Jesus. For example, Jesus reveals a God who so intensely loves us that he subjects himself to us. As incredible as it seems, Jesus subordinated himself to us in the ways listed below:

In the manner of his birth. Jesus came as King of kings and Lord of lords, but he was not born in a palace. He was born in a stable where animals saw him first and where the keepers of animals worshiped him first. The only thing memorable about Jesus' birthplace was that it needed to be deodorized.

The place of Christ's birth, however, was a deliberate choice. God condescended that he might lift up humanity. Jesus was not born as a king in a palace, but as a slave in a barn to give us a vision of humility and hope.

In the manner of his life. Jesus did not please himself when he put on a slave's apron and undertook to wash our dirty feet (John 13:4,5). Jesus did not live among us as one served, but as one who serves. He went about doing good. Jesus' every action, word, thought and prayer was in our behalf—for our good.

In the manner of his death. The cross was Jesus' ultimate subjection to us. At Calvary, Jesus emptied himself that we might be full (Philippians 2:8).

At the cross the enemies of Jesus unwittingly stated a truth when they said, "He saved others; himself he cannot save" (Matthew 27:42). That Jesus could not save himself is false in one sense. The Lord could have called legions of angels to deliver him from enemy hands. In another sense, however, Jesus could not save himself. He was the pledged mediator of mankind. If Jesus had saved himself, he would have frustrated redemption's plan, and we would remain unsaved.

Jesus' case was like the case of two men lost at sea with a one-man raft between them. This extreme case raises the question of whether one should save his life at the expense of the other or save the other's life at the expense of his own. Although Jesus agonized over his plight, he had no choice but to die that we might live.

In Jesus we see a God of unparalleled love. Many other aspects of God's nature would not be known, except for Jesus. The sincere God seeker needs no higher manifestation of Presence than Jesus.

The Church

In an age of television, the quick fix, and get-rich-quick thinking, people are too frenzied, jittery and restless to take the time to think.

Any workable formula for Presence also must include the church as one of its ingredients. The church began, not only because Jesus came as the presence of God among us "once upon a time," but because he remains as the living Presence among us still. When Jesus, after his resurrection, commanded his disciples to go into all the world preaching the gospel, he promised that he would be with them always, "even unto the end of the world" (Matthew 28:20). Because Jesus abides with his people, the honest God seeker always gives the church a place in his heart.

According to the New Testament scriptures, the church is also the temple of the Spirit. Paul wrote, "And what agreement hath the temple of God with idols? for ye are the temple of the living God . . ." (2 Corinthians 6:16). Upon obedience to the gospel, we are made a part of God's family, the church, where we find ourselves in the presence of God himself. God lives among Christians.

The church is also the place of communion. From the beginning, the church has congregated on the Lord's Day for the breaking of bread (Acts 20:7). When people of faith participate in fellowship of the Lord's Supper, the mood is joyful. Jesus comes so near during communion that God's people become influenced less by the world than by Presence.

Bible Reading and Prayer

In earlier chapters of this book, I established that Bible

study and prayer are indispensable ingredients of a sense of Presence. I will not, therefore, enlarge the thoughts here, except to say that we should develop the habit of *daily* study and prayer.

I want to encourage you not only to pray daily, but when you pray, remember God's promise to hear. Sense Divine Presence. If at first you find it difficult to feel God's nearness, don't give up. God is there, and in time you will progress to the point where your eye of faith will make him more real than anything you know.

When you read the Scriptures, never approach them with the thought, "God has spoken." Read with the thought, "God is speaking." God's Word is living and powerful. Read to know what God says to *you*.

Conclusion

I can see no hope for our unhappy and bewildered world except that which lies in a renewal of our awareness of God. In a similar way, I see no hope for the worldly church except that which exists in a sense of Presence.

Jesus was not born in a palace, but as a slave in a barn to give us a vision of humility and hope.

Just now, we are groping in darkness and sin. Let a certain holy ambition for God invade our souls, so that—content with nothing less than God himself—we rise above mediocrity; we shall find the light of life and joy.

God's will is not that he should remain hidden from us. Although God has concealed some things, he left nothing about himself unmarked. A sense of Presence is possible.

My prayer for you is that you may seek God, day and night, in season and out of season, when you work and when you play, and when you are awake and when you sleep.

A sense of Presence is your only hope for joy, peace and purpose in life. Pursue it with all your heart, soul, mind and strength.

Questions for Discussion

1. What is meditation? What makes meditation profitable?
2. What are some ways the world conditions us not to think or concentrate on spiritual things?
3. Why is it important to make time to think about God?
4. Why is familiarity with Jesus important to the God seeker?
5. How are God and Jesus the same? How are they different?
6. How did Jesus subject himself to us on the cross?
7. Why is the church important to the God seeker?
8. Why is the Lord's Supper important to the God seeker?
9. How should we pray? How should we read the Scriptures?
10. How do we know that God doesn't want to be vague to his people?